Telemarketing's
100 Do's & Don'ts

By The Staff
Of
Telemarketing® Magazine

TECHNOLOGY MARKETING CORPORATION®

One Technology Plaza • Norwalk • Connecticut • U.S.A. • 06854

To order this book call **(800) 243-6002**
For information call **(203) 852-6800**

cover design by Anna Miller

Publisher's Comments
&
Acknowledgements

We look at telemarketing as the renaissance of marketing. With the advent of high technology telecommunications equipment and services, telemarketing has become a primary cost-effective and efficient method of marketing. Combined with other marketing methods (direct mail, advertising, in-person sales call), it packs a punch unequalled in modern day business.

Today, companies must engage in telemarketing — either through in-house programs or by contracting with a service bureau — in order to gain and keep a competitive business advantage.

It has been said that telemarketing is an art as well as a science. *Telemarketing's 100 Do's & Don'ts* combines the best ideas of both disciplines to help expert and novice provide a better foundation for profitable and effective marketing. Our hope has also been to provide our readers guidance to prevent them from sustaining substantial losses as they start up a telemarketing operation.

It is in this spirit that the leading publisher in the telemarketing field presents *Telemarketing's 100 Do's & Don'ts*, as we continue to provide the best and most up-to-date information in this field for our valued readers.

The publisher wishes to gratefully acknowledge the dedicated assistance of Cheryl Lison, Kathleen Belmont and Linda Driscoll in making this book a reality.

Table of Contents

Introduction

You've heard that telemarketing can increase profitability and enhance your bottom line. You wonder if the success stories can possibly be true. Are there any shortcuts to telemarketing success? Are there any pitfalls that would stop you short of your goal?

Telemarketing, when done properly, is a complex discipline which combines technology and marketing methodologies with skillful human resources to increase sales, profits and productivity. One of telemarketing's most striking characteristics is the diversity of its applications. In an inbound mode, telemarketing draws clients to companies by incorporating toll-free telephone numbers in advertisements and other promotional literature. Outbound telemarketing is proactive; businesses actually reach out to customers via the telephone. In each telemarketing mode, flexible marketing strategies and adaptable technology can be powerful tools for creative managers.

This diversity may be frustrating for businesspeople seeking quick answers to their business problems: What works for one company won't necessarily work for another. In addition, telemarketing is an industry in which experience pays dividends, but it's an industry still so new, there are relatively few experienced managers. Those who have established successful operations tend to see the process that got them there as one of learning from experience, trial and error within plans of action designed to take advantage of technological advances and professional marketing techniques.

Successful managers emphasize the positive outcomes of their experience with systems that may not have worked the first time around. This optimistic and positive attitude undoubtedly contributes to the success of their programs. In the same spirit of optimistic enthusiasm, the TELEMARKETING® magazine staff has compiled this guide to help managers learn some of the basic rules for telemarketing success, based on interviews with tele-marketing managers as well as the wealth of material which has been contributed to TELEMARKETING® magazine.

Telemarketing is a complex interaction of several elements which will be covered in this guide. They include:

> *Management Commitment:* Without it, a telemarketing operation will fail. To even enter into a testing mode without top level support places an enormous obstacle in the road to success.
>
> *Planning:* The crucial phase of telemarketing development. You must evaluate where you are and where you want to go. How can you select the right road map if you don't know your destination?
>
> *Marketing Strategies:* Telemarketing is uniquely capable of supporting a variety of marketing strategies. It's like a beltway around a large city, offering you many approaches to your destination.
>
> *People:* Sales is your ultimate goal—and your telemarket-ing manager and telemarketing service reps will help you realize it. Since a major part of telemarketing expenses are related to staffing, you must carefully consider issues rang-ing from hiring to compensation, training and evaluation.
>
> *Ergonomics:* A link between your people and your tech-nology. How can you create an environment which makes people productive and equipment efficient? Telemarketing is

an intense, demanding activity and the work environment can increase stress or support productivity. Which do you think is going to make a healthier bottom line in the long run?

Telecommunications: The tools of telemarketing include the telephone system, automation, and data support. They put the "tele" in telemarketing.

Telemarketing Techniques: These are the implementation methods that will let your salespeople achieve your goals. They're based on common sense, require attention to detail, and pay off handsomely for large and small businesses doing inbound and outbound telemarketing.

The final word in our guide could as easily be the first word because it's the foundation for professionalism and the reputation of your business. ***Ethical Principles*** will perhaps be something you feel should go without saying, but it is important for the entire telemarketing industry, seasoned pros and newcomers alike, to understand and commit to practices that will earn customer respect and repeat business.

1

Chapter 1

Management Commitment

Telemarketing is a powerful sales tool, it isn't a quick fix for any business. Top management must be ready to support the long-term development of a telemarketing center which should be led by qualified people working under proper conditions, and with adequate technological and informational resources. Anything less than complete commitment will undermine the potential for success and invite failure.

Experienced, successful telemarketers are unanimous in their advice: Don't even think about introducing telemarketing unless you have top management approval. Telemarketing is a complex activity which will cut across department lines within an organization; therefore, management must set priorities and goals not only to launch the company's telemarketing effort but also to sustain it through the first months of implementation.

Telemarketing is a disciplined approach to sales which combines the efficiency of telecommunications with the productivity of marketing techniques. The discipline lends itself to hands-on learning because innovations can be quickly and precisely tested in the marketplace. The Do's and Don'ts of telemarketing are grounded in common sense and ethical business practices. There are no surprises or esoteric theories to consider, only the hard work and dedicated application which can make any business a success.

Each of these telemarketing Do's will be explored in this guide. Whether you are investigating an outside service vendor—or the feasibility of your own telemarketing center—you will need to give intelligent and serious consideration to each of these areas in order to realize maximum return on your investment.

DO:

• **Identify your goals and plan for a long-term commitment to develop an effective telemarketing management center.**
• **Develop a comprehensive marketing strategy.**
• **Consider human resource needs and developmental policies.**
• **Study and implement effective telemarketing techniques.**
• **Commit adequate telecommunications support for your operation.**
• **Provide sufficient data support to monitor your operation.**
• **Prepare a work environment that will create a productive atmosphere for your operation.**
• **Identify the evaluation techniques that will measure the achievement of your goals.**

The real test of management commitment will come into play when the impact of telemarketing begins to be felt throughout the organization. Most organizations resist change—and telemarketing promises significant change when it is done properly.

The first test of commitment may come as early as the planning stage when it may be apparent that some areas of the organization feel threatened by or are resisting the idea of telemarketing. A firm may successfully negotiate the planning phase, only to face disappointing profits or even losses during the first months of actual telemarketing. The telemarketing center may be off to a successful start only to have another area of the company sabotage high profit levels by refusing to cooperate with the new kid on the block.

In these instances, top management must step in to set priorities. The telemarketing manager of a medical instrumentation firm in California puts it this way. "Don't even think about telemarketing unless you have top management approval. Support and backing are necessary because there will inevitably be some issues of turf. You need someone at the top who will say, 'We want this to work and you will cooperate to make it work.'"

Another California telemarketer reinforces this observation. "In a large organization with several reporting routes to top management, there must be commitment to telemarketing or you will get caught in a quagmire of conflicting goals. In our case, we have to work from data bases of the branch banks, yet some of the branch managers were reluctant to have their customers called. My manager and the branch managers' supervisor were brought together by someone at a higher level who made the commitment to telemarketing. This helped and made a difference during the early stages of our telemarketing center."

The necessity for management commitment is no less important for a small business considering telemarketing than for a large one. A small business environment may be more easily able to nurture a new program because everyone can watch and foster it.

The marketing director of a direct mail business supply firm in Connecticut says that telemarketing is an option that small businesses should consider. "Look at some key pointers—average order size, repeat potential and market setting. If it looks as if there's a possibility that telemarketing would be effective, try some limited testing. Once a decision is made to go ahead with the project, commit resources, give attention to internal training and be flexible. It would be important for a company to stick with a new telemarketing program for at least a year—through all the ups and downs."

Chapter 2

Planning

Telemarketing is a powerful marketing tool but it is successful only when done with adequate planning, complete professionalism and creative marketing. The planning function is arguably the crucial phase in the development of a telemarketing operation. You and your management team must look beyond the appeal of telemarketing's notable successes to make sure you set up an operation that will work for you.

Don't fool yourself. Telemarketing is not an instant remedy for marketing frustrations. You cannot set up a telemarketing operation by plugging in a few telephones. Telemarketing requires planning, support, and management commitment to a new way of doing business.

In one sense, the planning phase of telemarketing is an evaluation phase. You must take a long, clear-eyed look at your current operation and determine the answers to several key questions before you decide to start a telemarketing operation. Will telemarketing meet your marketing needs? Can you generate new business with acceptable profit and loss? Can you define realistic goals achievable with telemarketing? Should you set up an in-house operation or use an outside agency?

DO:

• **Take the time to evaluate your current operation and expectations, using *Telemarketing's 100 Do's & Don'ts* as a guide.**

Whether they are involved in financial services or consumer products, telemarketers throughout the country offer similar advice—plan, plan, plan. Listen to their comments.

Banker in California—

Before you pick up the phone, clearly define your goals and how you're going to get there. Know how you are going to measure results. This may be relatively easy if you're selling a consumer item, but if you're selling a financial service, there are follow-up steps that must be documented.

Commercial realtor in Hawaii—

I've taken the time to plan this operation step by step. My managers were very enthusiastic and wanted to start up right away but I've resisted full-on telemarketing until all of the preliminary stages were complete.

Publisher in New York—

Plan your equipment and space for expansion, but start slowly. Hire a few people to work through your test period. Then, let the success of the program generate the hiring pace.

Insurance broker in Ohio—

Make sure you take the time to research what you want to accomplish. We've had a shaky start because we had lists of prospects but no telephone numbers. It's been very time-consuming to get this information. We should have invested in seminars or magazines and taken the time to plan our operation.

These are the voices of experience. Most of them are filled with optimism and success but the telemarketing manager in Ohio sounds tired, and a little frazzled. Be warned by her admonition.

In-house Or Outside Agency?

Part of your planning process will involve a look at whether you should set up an in-house operation or use the services of an outside agency, also known as a service bureau. Many companies use outside agencies to test the feasibility of telemarketing for their businesses. Other companies use an outside agency as a supplement to their own, in-house operations.

You must first establish your marketing objectives and construct a marketing plan. Then you can evaluate your needs against the following criteria.

Select the in-house option if you:
• **require repeated calling to a relatively small number of regular customers;**
• **need to convey a lot of technical or product information;**
• **expect to close, write orders, check inventories and schedule deliveries;**
• **can justify the ongoing requirement of high quality management and administrative costs;**
• **make telemarketing an integral part of the sales and marketing system.**

Select an outside agency if you:
• **need to have a large prospect pool carefully screened;**
• **will conduct several fragmented campaigns with different sales objectives;**
• **need short-term, intensive calling on an infrequent basis;**
• **can't use telephone equipment at maximum capacity.**

It's quite likely that you will decide that an outside agency can help you meet your marketing objectives, particularly if you decide to set up an outbound telemarketing operation. How do you find an effective, productive agency? You'll need to look carefully at several factors.

Experience. Business longevity doesn't guarantee success but a firm with a history of service can provide client references for you to check. Do so . . . then develop a list of likely candidates for more scrutiny.

Management orientation. Visit the consultants on your candidate list. You will be able to see the size and scope of their operations and you'll be able to assess their management philosophies. How do they develop an approach for a client? What are their primary considerations? How do they position telemarketing within a customer's overall marketing scheme?

Adequacy of resources. While you're visiting each agency, talk with the supervisors. They are the people who have immediate responsibility for the productivity, accuracy and quality of your program. While you're there, what are the working conditions for the TSRs (Telephone Sales Representatives)? Is the operation well organized? Are conditions crowded and frantic or is the environment adequately arranged and is the activity "humming"?

Performance of TSRs. In an outbound telemarketing program, the TSRs are critical to the success of your telemarketing program. Who are they? How long have they worked for the agency? How are they trained and how are they compensated? If you don't know the answers to these questions, you are signing a contract without reading the fine print.

Quality control. How does the agency monitor performance and ensure productivity over time?

Test vs. roll-out. A test will determine if an outbound telemarketing campaign will be cost-effective for you. Once a test is completed, the agency should guarantee that you will be supplied with detailed information that will let you decide whether to continue with a roll-out (full-blown) campaign.

Chapter 3

Marketing Strategy

Telemarketing applications offer businesspeople a tremendous range of options. Telemarketing can gather prospect information, qualify prospects, make appointments for field sales calls, take orders for new customers, cross-sell and up-sell products to existing customers. Although a telemarketing operation is a highly effective way to achieve a limited or specific goal, it is most effective when looked on as one of several approaches within an overall marketing plan. You will be able to maximize the effectiveness of each phase of the marketing effort if you consider telemarketing first and foremost as a marketing tool.

Marketing managers first look at the business environment to find ways to take advantage of the $80/20$ rule, i.e., 80 percent of the profits come from 20 percent of the customers. Once the high profit customers and primary market segments are identified, marketing executives can focus programs and sales efforts to reach them.

At the same time, marketing people must find ways to sell increasing numbers of new products. It's common for businesspeople to say that they market several products that didn't exist just a few years ago. All these new products require new customers who may exist in completely new markets.

DO:
• **Gain a competitive edge in this new marketing environment by segmenting your market.**
• **Integrate telemarketing into your overall marketing plan.**

In today's business environment, **you can gain a competitive edge if you segment your market.** You can generally divide your potential customers into four groups: (1) major accounts/large volume, (2) marginal accounts/large volume, (3) major accounts/small volume and (4) marginal accounts/small volume.

Major accounts/large volume, group 1, are usually personal sales targets. Typically these accounts are in a city, have significant dollar potential, won't waste time by talking with sellers unless they're interested in the product, and have the potential for long-term relationships. Most sellers gravitate toward this customer group—and stay there!

What about the rest of the potential customer base? Group 4 offers little potential in the way of sales, so it's unlikely that you could justify any major expense in trying to reach it. However, telemarketing may be your best way to handle the sales effort for groups 2 and 3.

Your company may offer a product which may be profitable but doesn't have the volume potential to justify the attention of a personal sales call. Specialty or seasonal products may fall into this category and could become the focus of a targeted telemarketing campaign to your large accounts.

The other side of the coin, major products to marginal accounts, includes selling your products to small or geographically remote accounts.

Of course, don't overlook the ways in which the telemarketing effort can support the sales effort to the first group. The field sales staff can be freed to conduct visits that end in sales if a trained telemarketing staff stands behind them, prospecting, profiling and qualifying leads.

Telemarketing not only lowers the cost of sales to new customers, it will help you maintain market penetration and protect market share. How? **You must integrate telemarketing into your overall marketing plan.**

The Marketing Mix

Telemarketing is an important addition to the marketing tools that help companies sell their products. Typically, those tools include advertising, public relations, direct mail, sales promotion and market research. These activities are all geared to bringing Mohammed to the mountain, bringing customers to companies in order to save the enormous expense of trying to reach every potential customer in person.

An inbound telemarketing operation supports this marketing activity. Potential customers who respond to the persuasion of a promotional or advertising piece are drawn to the company thanks to toll-free numbers and the efficiency of the telephone. This is sometimes called direct response marketing or reactive marketing.

An outbound telemarketing operation, however, actually brings the mountain to Mohammed, enabling the company to travel door-to-door without the expense of leaving the office. Outbound telemarketing is also known as direct marketing or proactive marketing.

In order to take full advantage of these benefits, however, you must have a comprehensive marketing plan that coordinates each element of the marketing mix. The guidelines are simple but don't underestimate the analysis and planning that you must invest in order to maximize the return on your marketing dollars.

DO:

• **Conduct sufficient market research to define your customer base and determine what your customers want. If you don't have this expertise within your company, hire professional help.**
• **Develop a concentrated, systematic approach that will reach each of your target markets with maximum impact.**

• Try to use telemarketing as a bandage to quick fix weak or ill-conceived marketing campaigns.

Integrating The Marketing Mix

Tips For A Direct Response Campaign

So you're convinced that telemarketing might help the introduction of your new product. Let's assume it's a computer enhancement of some sort—technical but not overly complicated. We'll also assume that you're using a telemarketing staff in conjunction with field sales reps.

Who's going to handle the customer calls and how will they screen the likely leads? What kind of follow-up will you provide? Where will you advertise? Will you set up an outbound operation to prospect a customer list or will you rely on inbound sales in response to your advertising? Will the telemarketing staff close the sale or does your product warrant field sales follow-up?

Let's sort out these questions and handle each element of the campaign in order.

DO:

• Plan an advertising program which will generate your sales leads.
• Plan your program of lead qualification.
• Have your field staff poised to act quickly to convert the leads into satisfied customers.

In order to effectively **plan an advertising program which will generate your sales leads,** you must evaluate media in light of telemarketing requirements. You must know the inquiry volume potential since it will affect production and staffing requirements, phone facilities and the ultimate cost of the program.

All advertising media has a measurable effective life. The effective life of the advertising media you use has a direct effect on the volume of sales leads generated at any point during the campaign. For example, consider the difference between the four to six weeks of a postcard pack ad and the three-year life of an industrial purchasing directory.

As a rule, there are no partial steps in this kind of telemarketing program. It's a total commitment. Although you should start the program slowly, perhaps in one geographic location, if you expect to market your product nationally, anticipate a 12-hour day (8:00 a.m. to 8:00 p.m. EST) to match business hours on both the east and west coasts.

Consider the design of your advertising as well. What's the most important element? The 800 number. It will drive your graphic designer crazy, but your 800 number should be prominently displayed. People call toll-free numbers because they have an immediate need for information in order to make a buying decision. The 800 number promises immediate assistance, so by making it easy for the potential customer to find the number, you're making it easier for your staff to secure a sale.

Plan your program of lead qualification. This second element of your direct response campaign sets up the quick response mechanism for the rest of the sales process. You must determine in advance what information will qualify the lead and how the information will be processed and given priority.

After determining what information will be necessary to qualify your leads, you must determine how much product training will be necessary for the TSR to adequately accomplish this task. Don't skimp on this area of preparation. You may not have another chance at this potential customer and you don't want to lose a sale because your sales rep couldn't understand the customer's needs.

You also must set up a procedure which will assign and handle priority leads. The procedure may be as simple as penciling notations on a pre-printed form or as complex as an interactive computer system. Your choice is a matter of time and cost versus the information you need to ensure success.

Immediate follow-up, usually a mailing of literature or a letter summarizing the conversation, is a good practice. This also confirms each inquiry call and serves as a bridge to the final step in the direct response campaign, the sales call.

Have your field staff in place, poised to act quickly to convert the leads into satisfied customers. It's essential that the field salespeople understand the importance of immediate response to a lead qualified through a direct response campaign.

The effectiveness of an 800 number is the degree to which it satisfies the customer's immediate need for information in order to make a buying decision. Thus, the salesperson can be assured that the customer is ready to act. This kind of lead cannot fall to the bottom of the in-basket. After you have introduced the campaign, you must sustain interest and underline the importance of the program by publicizing results and holding people accountable for the follow-up and conversion of the leads.

Chapter 4

People

At the heart of the definition of telemarketing is sales and at the heart of the sales process are people. How do you find the manager who will effectively lead your telemarketing operation? How does the manager find and keep communicators who will be productive day in and day out?

When you begin the search for the right people, you are starting a process that is as critical as selecting your phone system. Since telemarketing is a union of technology and people, you must look for your people as carefully as you do your equipment.

DO:

• **Create a profile of your ideal telemarketing manager.**
• **Create a profile of your ideal telemarketing representative.**
• **Let your telemarketing manager take the time to screen and recruit ideal representatives.**
• **Commit adequate resources to training your people.**

Profile: The Telemarketing Manager

The tremendous expansion of the telemarketing industry in the 1980s demands people who are capable of managing a telemarketing operation. The combination of skills and abilities that characterize a telemarketing manager would be difficult enough to find in any business area. Trying to find the combination in someone with experience in the still youthful telemarketing industry often seems impossible.

Consider the variety of hats a telemarketing manager wears: market researcher, first-line supervisor, data base builder, list manager, sales strategist. These roles require communication and people skills, analytical and quantitative skills, creativity, imagination, and technical understanding. The most important attribute of an effective telemarketing manager, however, is an understanding of telemarketing. To ensure the success of a telemarketing operation:

DO:

• **Hire a manager who understands the unique demands of telemarketing.**

DON'T:

• **Hire anyone who hasn't spent time on the phones.**

When all of the sophisticated technology and data analysis is stripped away, the key person in the sales equation is the communicator or telephone sales representative. Telemarketing managers will be effective leaders only if they can identify the pressures and demands their communicators face. If they act on that identification, they will treat their people well as human beings—perhaps the single, most important requirement for a successful telemarketing operation.

Hire a manager who understands the unique demands of telemarketing. Telemarketing is a specialized discipline that combines technology and sales in a highly productive and efficient manner. As the leader of a management team, you should develop a checklist which profiles your "ideal" telemarketing manager. This can be done only if you are clear about the goals you want the telemarketing operation to achieve. If the goals are defined, the telemarketing manager profile will fall into place and can be used as a guide during interviews and reference checks.

There are several areas which may form the basis for the interview checklist. The importance of each area will vary from company to company, depending on management's goals.

Telemarketing skills. What are candidates' criteria for measuring performance, for evaluating staff, for training staff, for managing lists, for selecting equipment? While each of these areas is important, particularly probe the candidates' attitudes toward staff training and supervision. Do they understand that a TSR is productive for four hours? That the needs of a second shift person are different from those of a person who starts at 9:00 a.m.?

Management skills. What kind of operation has each candidate run before? Was he involved in start-up? Did she intervene to save a failing operation? How long did each candidate work for another employer? Did he or she groom a successor (the mark of a good manager)?

Technological background. What is each candidate's attitude toward computers and automation? Beware of the candidate who thinks computers are the only answer. In a start-up situation, a manual system is more flexible. This allows the manager to introduce technology when the system is ready—not design a system to meet the demands of the computer.

Marketing and sales skills. Do the candidates understand the principles of integrating telemarketing into the overall marketing mix? Will any of the candidates be able to establish the telemarketing staff as an important component of an integrated field sales/telemarketing team?

Industry perspective. Candidates who understand the industry as a whole will probably bring a higher level of professionalism to your company. Are they aware of the DMA's Guidelines for Telephone Marketing? [See Appendices for complete set of DMA Guidelines.] Are they familiar with legislative and regulatory efforts that crop up in various areas of the country? Will the professionalism of any of the candidates enhance your reputation with your customers and competitors?

If you find someone who has good qualifications, yet lacks specific telemarketing experience, invest in that candidate's potential: Plan to have the potential manager spend the first one or two months working in your phone room. If this isn't possible, proceed with caution and **don't hire anyone who hasn't spent time on the phones.**

This admonition is based on the experience of many businesses that tried telemarketing and failed. Everyone's familiar with the telephone. Unfortunately, this leads people to the conclusion that everyone—or anyone—can manage a telemarketing center.

Top managers of a large corporation in the Northeast wanted to develop a major outbound telemarketing operation. Their commitment to technological support was enormous but they didn't make a similar commitment to telemarketing. The initial managers (who were systems analysts, not telemarketers) knew a lot about data, but they didn't understand the dynamics of the phone room. They didn't understand sales or how to motivate people.

Consequently, the telemarketers were trained to use the computers but not trained to sell and they weren't productive. Moreover, they felt as if they were part of the automated machine rather than the vital component of the sales transaction. As their productivity decreased, phone room profits decreased and ultimately people were laid off as the telemarketing operation failed to be profitable.

Telemarketing professionals could point to several mistakes

which should have been addressed, and which might have been addressed by an experienced telemarketing manager. As originally planned, the operation was much too large. A well-managed tele-marketing room is tightly run—new stations are added only as the system is pushed to its limit by the productivity of the TSR staff.

The emphasis on computer rather than sales training might also have been corrected by a telemarketer who would have known how to create a cohesive sales unit. The telemarketing manager of a highly successful lead qualification unit for a publisher in the Northeast talks about her ability to be both "mother hen" and boss. She's able to demand a high performance level because the staff knows that she's always available to listen and encourage. This is a pattern she's observed in other successful telemarketing managers—both male and female.

This ability is a direct result of experience in the phone room. "As a manager, you've got to understand that it's the most tedious job in the world. TSRs face constant rejection. You can only understand this if you've done it; and if you've done it, you'll respect the people you manage." In short, the telemarketing manager must be a people-person, perhaps a little flaky, certainly able to help staff laugh off rejection and stress. People must be treated like human beings, not data entry devices.

Profile:
The Telephone Sales Representative

TSRs are the front line. For many customers, they are your company. Their skills can make or break a sale and their productivity is at the heart of a profitable telemarketing operation. An ad for recruits might read like an impossible dream:

WANTED: The telephone sales representative, a.k.a., the TSR, the communicator, the customer service representative. Must like to talk on the phone. Must have good listening skills. Must have an articulate, persuasive voice. Must be able to ignore rejection. Must be able to sit still for four hours, but project enthusiasm and energy at the same time.

Impossible to find this person? Not if top management is committed to providing complete support for the company's human resources and if the telemarketing manager is effective in molding that support into a telemarketing team.

DO:

- **Take the time to find the right people.**
- **Make sure the employees will value working for you.**

DON'T:

- **Think that you have to cope with constant turnover. Successful operations have people with two to four years' experience—it's possible to create a viable, long-term telemarketing team.**

Take the time to find the right people. You are investing in potential supervisors and managers as well as telephone reps. There are various methods for recruiting and screening TSRs. Whether a telemarketing manager uses a point system or some other guide, some basic attributes and attitudes underlie the search.

Talking Skills. The TSR who can move along without pauses will remain in control of the conversation, even while maintaining a friendly and agreeable tone. "Do you like to talk on the phone?" should be one of the first questions you ask a candidate. If this answer is anything but unequivocally "yes," stop the proceedings as quickly as possible.

Listening Skills. Because the sales situation requires the mental agility to cope with unexpected responses, the TSR must have good listening skills in order to respond to the customer.

Voice. A TSR must convey both authority and respect, using a tone that will establish rapport by saying "I have the right to talk with you as an equal, but I will not harass you."

Speaking Style. Cultured, folksy, crisp, regional dialect? Each of these factors will come into play depending on the product or area of the country that is targeted. While the script is an important component in creating an unstudied and clear presentation, TSRs can modulate the conversation if they are confident and positive about their own professionalism.

Psychological Orientation. Three components really work together to make someone an outstanding TSR. The right training program can enhance attributes, but the super employee will come into the job with these qualities:

1. *Confidence.* For four to five hours, an effective TSR may have to deal with rejection 85 percent of the time. The ability to go on to the next call, without internalizing a "no" response, is an important factor for maintaining productivity.

2. *Customer orientation.* TSRs should understand that each call is an important sales opportunity. TSRs who value the company and product will therefore structure and deliver presentations that meet customers' needs.

3. *Motivation.* Many people who get involved in telemarketing are looking for an opportunity to earn money. If people are productive, telemarketing will pay off for them. Look for people who have a strong work ethic. They will have the stamina to work through the stresses of the job and reap the financial rewards.

It isn't enough that you find people with the skills you need—they must be motivated to use them. **Make sure that the employees will value working for you.** The telephone reps are often a customer's only contact with your company so make sure that they are proud to work for you.

A telemarketing manager can set up part of the screening process to establish the benefits of working for the company. This is where management commitment is really important—these must be real, not imaginary benefits. Thorough training, excellent supervision, adequate compensation, and a work environment that eases stress and promotes efficiency are all components of successful telemarketing operations. Make sure potential TSRs know that these benefits will be theirs if they work for you.

Don't think that you have to cope with constant turnover. Successful operations have people with two to four years' experience. It is possible to create a viable, long-term telemarketing team when people value their employment and the opportunity to fulfill their potential. Each employee may have a different goal, but whether it's money or advancement within the organization, the benefit will accrue to your company.

Recruiting And Screening

Hiring decisions are often made on the basis of subjective observations. While no business consistently can afford to hire the wrong people, in the fast paced world of telemarketing, incorrect decisions have immediate impact on the telemarketing center. Therefore, managers must try to be accurate in their initial assessment of employee potential.

Fortunately, there are several strategies that can help a manager identify and hire productive telephone representatives.

DO:

• **Establish a way to quickly identify good telephone personalities.**
• **Set up an interview process that will convince the candidate that telephone representatives are important to the organization.**

DON'T:

• **Try to hire telephone representatives against the same criteria as other sales employees.**

If telemarketing managers take the time to create a profile of ideal telephone representatives, they will quickly see that the voice and telephone personality of candidates are a key screening device. Therefore, they **establish a way to quickly identify good telephone personalities.** The best screening device is, of course, at hand. In newspaper or other ads, direct candidates to call to set up appointments. The manager, or a trained assistant, can screen these calls and determine if each candidate's voice and diction are adequate. This is a check on the basics—if a candidate has the raw materials, schedule an interview.

The in-person interview should be designed to provide consistent, comparative information about candidates. **Don't try to hire telephone representatives against the same criteria as other sales employees.** You do want to hire them against consistent criteria which are critical to the telemarketing sales environment.

A typical field salesperson has a great deal of independence and autonomy. In contrast, the telephone salesperson is the member of a telemarketing team. Although there are individual goals and standards, the unit or team often works toward a shared goal.

Therefore, a telemarketing manager must be looking for evidence of team work and a cooperative attitude.

Another difference between field and telephone sales is time. In virtually the same amount of time that a field salesperson is going through conversational preliminaries, telemarketers have to break the ice and close the sale. Look for signs that a candidate can quickly move to the main point of a conversation. For example, ask an open-ended question that requires a candidate to summarize the reasons he or she would be a good employee. Does the answer demonstrate quick thinking and the ability to analyze the information you've already shared?

The final function of the interview process is to **convince the candidate that telephone representatives are important to the organization.** One rationale for administering sales aptitude or creativity tests is that they reinforce the selective part of the process. Some telemarketers use the testing as part of their objective criteria and use a follow-up interview with strong candidates as the reinforcing element.

Since telemarketing organizations frequently promote from within, a careful hiring process may have an impact beyond the profitability of the telemarketing center. The candidate who feels that a great deal of care went into the hiring decision will likely feel that similar care goes into training and evaluation. Ultimately, the candidate-employee who feels valued will be willing to perform at a high level of productivity.

Training

Enthusiastic management may think that the sooner a new employee is on the phone, the sooner the profits will increase. This is shortsighted; telemarketing is a sufficiently complex activity to warrant meticulous and thoughtful training.

If you've already made the commitment to recruit and hire your telephone reps properly, realize that it's important to protect that investment. Just as you wouldn't expect equipment to work unless properly installed, look at the orientation and training of TSRs as their proper installation into the organization. Common sense—and a few tested guidelines—can lead the way.

DO:

• **Give solid product training—before you give any telemarketing training.**
• **Cover general sales orientation, with special emphasis on telemarketing sales.**
• **Let new employees learn from experienced telemarketers.**
• **Set up role-playing opportunities.**

DON'T:

• **Limit training to the first day on the job.**

Give solid product training—before you give any telemarketing training. It's confusing to learn the two at one time. This part of the training will vary according to the complexity of the product or product line.

The amount of training also will vary with the degree of automated support that is available to the representatives. A highly automated system may provide on-line information which will enhance the knowledge base and allow the rep to sell more products. Note, however, that the telephone rep then must be trained to work with the computer system.

Cover general sales orientation, with special emphasis on telemarketing sales. It's worthwhile to make sure your telephone reps have solid training in sales techniques as well as an understanding of the general sales environment.

Then, make sure your reps understand telemarketing as a sales process. How does telemarketing fit into the direct marketing picture? What is the role of your telemarketing operation: lead qualification, field sales support, account management, or sales, sales, sales?

Let new employees learn from experienced telemarketers. This may be one of the best ways to introduce new employees to the crux of telemarketing activity. By listening to an experienced telemarketer handle objections, break through call screeners or encourage positive decisions, the new rep can anticipate his or her own responses.

The new rep can also learn about handling rejection and staying "up" after repeated phone calls. Perhaps the most important thing the experienced rep can convey, however, is the sense of teamwork that is a hallmark of successful operations. If the new rep can learn about group goals and performance levels, he or she can internalize a standard for individual performance.

Set up role-playing opportunities. Role-playing sessions are very important because you can instill exactly the kind of habits that will make for a successful TSR. Role-playing gives you a chance not only to teach technique, but also to instill confidence. Use a tape recorder to help TSRs evaluate their own presentations.

Consider the first weeks on the phones as an extension of the training period. **Don't limit training to the first day on the job.** As new reps assimilate information, practice technique and develop confidence, you can increase productivity by reinforcing good habits and discouraging bad ones. Supervisors should carefully monitor performance, and set up frequent feedback sessions to promote learning. This is also a time to build confidence so don't assign a new product list to new reps. Let them work targeted leads during the early phase of their employment because this is a critical time to develop positive attitudes. Remember, the investment you make in training will have direct payoff in long-term productivity and employee loyalty.

Incentives And Motivation

After committing so many resources to hiring and training the right people, why do some companies feel they can live with constant turnover and employee burnout? A good manager will want to keep good people—is it an impossible task?

"Let's be clear," says a telemarketing trainer with an established service vendor in Connecticut, "TSRs are already highly motivated—with their own reasons, not yours. What the successful manager can and must do is create and maintain an environment in which employees can motivate themselves."

Next door in New York, two telemarketing managers echo this theme. "I'm constantly on the floor, patting heads, getting people to laugh. I worked the phone as a TSR and a supervisor. I know that this is an incredibly difficult job and it's important that I keep my people 'up.' Right now I'm looking for some cartoons to put up on the wall. I want people to have a reason to put a smile into their voices."

Cartoons and pats on the head? Is this the stuff of long-term employee commitment? Perhaps. Over the last 10 years telemarketers have learned that a humanistic approach to telemarketing is much more successful than a production-oriented approach. If you want to duplicate the success of these telemarketers,

DO:

• **Set up an equitable compensation structure.**
• **Give your telemarketing supervisors and managers flexibility to design incentive strategies.**

• **Create an environment that makes expectations clear and provides feedback that enhances performance.**

DON'T:

• **Forget that people respond to recognition beyond compensation and incentives.**

The compensation structure for the telemarketing center staff will vary from company to company. Make sure you **set up a compensation structure that will give people a chance to earn money on equitable terms with the rest of your employees.**

Customer service reps who handle inbound calls may be on salary. Telephone reps doing outbound work may be on commission, salary or base-plus-bonus and this can change from campaign to campaign. Lead qualification, for example, is not the time to have people on commission—you'll get lots of leads, but they will not be quality leads.

You'll want to be sure that the compensation package for the telemarketing staff is equitable in terms of the rest of the sales or marketing team. But within the telemarketing area, the primary concern will be with day-to-day, hour-to-hour, call-to-call incentive. At this level, the true worth of the experienced telemarketing manager shines.

Give your telemarketing supervisors and managers flexibility to design incentive strategies that will meet the motivational needs of their employees.

"I used to work phones and I have a room full of junk that proves I was good," says one manager. He's running a field sales support operation for a contractors' supply house and trying to increase the level of new product sales by the telemarketing customer service reps. "I'm constantly setting up contests, quick games for my people. It's not the prize itself, it's the winning that counts."

Very simple rewards like a candy bar for most calls per hour can motivate an entire group to increase productivity. The recurrent theme is spontaneity and fairness. Everyone should feel there is a chance to "win"—if the prize is too expensive or the rules too elaborate, the average performer may not be motivated and the top salespeople may become too serious about the goal.

Create an environment that makes expectations clear and provides feedback that enhances performance. The overall work environment is very important for retaining committed employees. Positive feedback reinforces the attainment of goals. "I make sure that our department goals are clearly stated and that the reps understand how they support that goal. This is a general principle of good management, but it's especially important in telemarketing where our goals change so rapidly to meet the demands of the market," notes a telemarketing banker in California.

Individual development and opportunity for promotion will also create a positive environment. Good managers provide sales communication training, coaching and feedback, helping TSRs measure their performance against the standards for the department.

A wholesale distributor in South Carolina spends "a heck of a lot of money training people" because it helps people to develop their full potential. "Show me one company that's outgrowing another and I'll show you the company that's doing something with people that the other company is not doing," says the company president.

The incentive lesson for telemarketers to learn is that people want to be treated like human beings, not robots. People want a manager to listen to their frustrations and suggestions and they want to be recognized for their contributions. **Don't forget that people respond to recognition beyond compensation and incentives.** They respond to the deeper, human recognition of trusting,

respecting, listening, keeping promises, training, coaching, prais-
ing, liking and caring. In short, people respond to a wholesome
work atmosphere in which they are valued employees.

Evaluation—And Termination

Even after you have made every effort to set up a recruiting
and hiring process that will identify the strongest possible pool of
candidates, chances are some of the new hires will not be productive—even after the benefit of your superior training program.

The best remedy is quick release of the new hires. This can
be accomplished only if you set clearly defined performance goals
and create an evaluative structure to measure them.

DO:

• **Analyze the performance requirements of your operation and
define these standards before new hires begin.**
• **Meet with employees at regular intervals. Review performance and establish written goals.**

DON'T:

• **Allow an employee to continue if it's clear he or she cannot
meet the minimum accepted level of performance for your telemarketing unit.**

This advice may seem to be a return to a production line
mentality. The harsh reality, however, is that productivity is the
bottom line for a telemarketing operation—and players who can't
contribute to that productivity become a liability to the entire
team. They know it and the team knows it. The earlier a manager
can identify people who lack the necessary ingredients for success,

the sooner he or she can concentrate time and money on the people who deserve it.

Field Sales/Telemarketing Cooperation

Whether you initially introduce telemarketing into the sales process as a support system for the regular sales team, or you plan to establish telemarketing as an alternative sales operation for certain kinds of accounts, you must ensure the cooperation of each staff. An "us-them" situation will benefit no one. The telemarketing staff will be isolated from the experience of the regular staff and the experienced staff won't be able to make full use of the telemarketing support for their efforts.

A sincere and dedicated sales manager can compromise a new telemarketing operation because he or she relies on years of experience and places more value on the field sales force. You must avoid this situation.

DON'T:

• **Place the telemarketing sales force in a lower position than the field sales force.**
• **Contrive a revolution.**
• **Set up a territory/compensation conflict.**

Telemarketers must be positioned at the same organizational level as the field sales representatives. You must avoid the negative impact on the morale of the telemarketing force which would occur if people in the company perceive the telemarketers in a "lower" position. You also want to avoid the situation in which telemarketers themselves internalize the negative image, consequently setting less than high performance standards for themselves.

While you must protect the status of the telemarketers, you also must be sensitive to the needs of the existing staff. **Don't contrive a revolution.** Plan a phase-in period. Sudden or insensitive replacement of field sales staff with telemarketing people will create conflict and tension which will affect the productivity of the whole company.

A corollary of organizational equity in terms of the telemarketing staff's relationship to the field sales staff is the need to deal with compensation equity. **Don't set up a territory/compensation conflict.** During the introductory phases of the telemarketing operation, make sure you have set up a mechanism that recognizes the telemarketing contribution to the final sale. Anticipate the possibility that as the telemarketing operation becomes more aggressive, the field sales force will feel that its territory is being invaded. Prepare for splitting compensation until final market integrity is established and recognized.

The benefits of cooperative and coordinated field and telemarketing sales are illustrated by the experience of a college textbook publisher in California. About five years ago, both the telemarketing center and the field sales force were set up at the direction of the publisher's parent company. With management commitment as a key support, sensitive issues of turf were resolved and the sales team was established.

Telemarketing staff is kept as close as possible to the criteria for field sales staff, that is, issues of professionalism and overall job prestige are equal. The in-house reps have autonomous territories which supplement the national sales effort by handling geographically isolated or very small accounts where the sales volume can't justify personal sales visits.

Because the telemarketing reps have autonomous territories, they have compensation packages similar to the field sales reps. Although some of the sales strategies are different, there are more similarities than differences in the sales interactions of the two groups.

The telemarketing manager notes that the coordinated sales forces have yielded a special bonus for the company. "We hire young, out-of-college professionals, who are interested in sales or publishing, for our telemarketing operation. We're discovering that the in-house center is becoming a feeder to field sales. We're able to put highly trained and experienced sales reps into the field—and they aren't threatened by the telemarketing operation! This is proving [to be] a real plus for our overall sales effort."

Chapter 5

Ergonomics

Telemarketing brings technology and human resources together. And successful interaction between people and their machines has been proven to be vital to increased productivity. Ergonomics is an area of study concerned with molding the four major workplace factors—people, product, process, place—into an integrated, productive whole. The products a TSR uses, and how and where they are used, can be the deciding elements in the competitive marketing arena. Effective use of ergonomic advances is one of the best ways to protect your largest telemarketing investment because personnel-related expenses typically account for 85-95 percent of telemarketing costs.

As a telemarketing manager, you should understand the three major ways the work environment can affect employee performance. You then can provide the best possible environment for your people, often with relatively little expense.

DO:

• **Make the physical environment as comfortable for your people as it is for your machines.**
• **Make the environment psychologically supportive to ensure maximum effectiveness.**
• **Make the environment motivationally supportive to ensure maximum productivity.**

DON'T:

• **Think you can skimp on the work environment.**

Modern telecommunications equipment often requires environmentally controlled rooms. Systems will fail if certain physical requirements are not met. The needs of TSRs deserve equal consideration if you want to have a telemarketing operation that runs at maximum productivity. **Make the physical environment as comfortable for your people as it is for your machines.**

Comfort. As you manage your energy-related activities, make sure that you allow for the comfort of your TSRs. Temperature should be set between 70 and 72°F with relative humidity at a maximum 59 percent in summer and 49 percent during the winter. Air should be kept in constant circulation.

Lighting. You can save up to 5–8 watts per square foot by combining overhead and task lighting. Not only does this arrangement benefit the TSR by focusing the light at the task level where it's needed, it cuts down on air conditioning costs in the summer by reducing the amount of heat that the overhead lights generate.

Noise. Perhaps the most disruptive environmental factor is noise. In a high-tech office, the sounds of printers and copiers, phones and people can combine to produce so much auditory confusion the TSR cannot concentrate on the sale. Acoustic panels on ceiling and wall surfaces, specialized carpeting, and phones with lights instead of bells cut down on the noise pollution of modern offices. Your goal is to keep noise below 85 decibels (and if you note that a good printer will create this much noise, you can see how quickly the problem can be compounded). One of the most direct ways to cut down on noise levels is to use acoustic panels to absorb noise and reduce sound transmission from one office to another. Also, headsets with noise canceling features help insulate both the TSR and the customer from background noise.

Make the environment psychologically supportive to ensure maximum effectiveness. The factors that contribute to physical comfort may also have an effect on the psychological reactions that people have to their work environment.

Privacy. It's extremely important to provide "offices." Telemarketers will tell you that each TSR needs an office—conducting business under the intense level of telemarketing activity can quickly degenerate into a boiler room atmosphere if people are not separated from each other. It's equally important, however, that offices not be isolated. A good workstation design has three walls, 48″–54″ high. This establishes privacy, but keeps the environment open and spacious.

Spaciousness. While you want to create a feeling of privacy you also want to have an overall atmosphere that is spacious. Workstations need to be slightly larger than the average for office workers, since you don't want TSRs to feel trapped by their three walls. In addition, the workstation often must accommodate not only phone but CRT, terminal, reference manuals and other items. The workstation design should make all of these tools easily accessible so the ongoing telemarketing activity is not interrupted.

Colors. You may need expert help to plan the color scheme for your telemarketing center. Usually, neutral color tones are used since they have a calming effect: Telemarketing activity is emotionally charged on its own. Avoid red since it's generally associated with anger, but don't be afraid to select colors that will keep people "up" without tiring them over the long haul.

Make the environment motivationally supportive to ensure maximum productivity. Adaptations that recognize the individuality of your TSRs, that recognize their "humanness" can go a long way toward increasing the motivation of your staff. Thus, it's a good idea to let people personalize their work space. Photographs, small plants or other personal items let people identify with their space. In turn, they feel comfortable and supported by the environment which contributes to good morale.

You may also be able to enhance morale by considering the impact of physical location on group compatibility. The location of workstations can reduce personality conflicts or can induce peer support and reinforcement. What are the personal interactions among your TSRs? Could you improve morale if you clustered workstations or set up challenge teams?

Physical and environmental factors can have a far-reaching effect on the total performance of your telemarketing center. Think about it. If, as we say, the customer can hear the smile in a TSR's voice, doesn't it make sense to do everything possible to encourage that smile? Someone whose eyes ache, back or head hurts, who's too cold or too hot, or who is distracted by the sounds of 20 other phone conversations is going to have difficulty paying attention, never mind smiling! **Don't think you can skimp on the work environment.** The customer may not be able to see you, but if the TSRs are uncomfortable or distracted by the physical environment, the customer will hear the message, "loud and clear."

Chapter 6

Telecommunications In Action

Telecommunications technology, blended with savvy marketing by competent, professional telemarketers is a key to business success. In this section, we'll look at technology issues: The Telephone System, Automation and Data Support. These are the major areas that combine to put the "tele" in telemarketing.

Telemarketing centers don't need to be completely automated to be efficient and cost-effective. However, telemarketing is such a labor intensive activity, even moderate automation can produce a big pay-back.

Another payoff for the telemarketing center is the evaluation and needs analysis which accompany telecommunications decisions. Whether your management team is considering computer support or a new telephone system or a new software package, your first step should be a comprehensive review of the current operation. This review will point out weak areas in the telemarketing operation, give direction for future growth and lead to new, more profitable ways of doing business.

Three themes are consistent in this section:

DO:

• **Thoroughly investigate the technology.**
• **Involve end users, as much as possible, in the investigation and purchase process.**

DON'T:

• **Let technology set the pace. Make sure the telemarketing center needs determine the technology.**

The Telephone System

Telemarketers know that the telephone is the most important piece of equipment in their offices. Before the deregulation of the telecommunications industry, decisions about telephone systems were relatively simple—shall we call Ma Bell today or tomorrow? Today's business planner, considering a new or retooled phone system, faces a much more complicated decision, but it's one that an informed manager can make by following a few basic guidelines.

DO:

• **Master the vocabulary. Telephone systems offer a range of options which are described by new terms and acronyms. You'll need to learn them in order to ask questions.**
• **Ask questions . . . of manufacturers or retailers and of the end users of their products or services.**

DON'T:

• **Be impatient.**

Ignorance may be bliss—but not when deciding on a telephone system. There's no substitute for informed "shopping" and there's probably no other way to begin to be informed than to **master the vocabulary** of the new telephone technology. Here you go:

ACD—Automatic Call Distributor. A machine that automatically manages and controls incoming calls, evenly sending calls to the telephone rep who has been idle the longest, answering and queuing calls during busy periods, playing recorded messages for delayed callers. Automatically overflows calls to a secondary group if they are delayed too long and provides management reports on the call activity. Today's ACDs can provide management with detailed reports regarding agents and program activity. The ACD can stand alone or be integrated with a PBX (see PBX).

Add-on Conference. A telephone feature that allows an additional internal party to be added to a CO (central office) line for a three-way conference (see CO).

AGC—Automatic Gain Control. A feature built into the amplifier system of a telephone headset that ensures that incoming signal levels do not exceed a fixed pressure, or amplifies signal levels that are weak.

All Call. A telephone feature that gives a user the ability to communicate with all system stations at one time.

ANI—Automatic Number Identification. Part of a PBX management report which allows the phone company to generate a bill broken down by telephone number extension for individual accountability.

Analog Signals. Voice signals.

ARS—Automatic Route Selection. A switching system that chooses the least costly path from available owned or leased circuits. It is transparent to callers (also see LCR).

Attendant Reversion. Calls ring back to attendant when a transferred call goes unanswered.

Audio Conferencing. The simplest and most available form of teleconferencing in which three or more people communicate simultaneously in conference style, by telephone, in real time without visual aid.

Automatic Answering Machine. Plays and records single messages.

Automatic Dialing Recorded Message Programs (ADRMP). A machine that dials a preprogrammed telephone number and plays an automatic recording—normally a sales pitch.

Automatic Dialers. A telephone feature or stand alone device capable of storing phone numbers in memory for easier access. (Not to be confused with ADRMPs.)

Automatic Privacy On CO Lines. Prevents a third party from entering into a call unless allowed to do so on controlling station. (See CO heading.)

Automatic Redial. A telephone feature which permits the last number dialed to be automatically dialed again at the push of one button.

Barge Out Device. A machine that announces the same outgoing message to all callers.

Baud. A unit of signaling speed in telegraphic code. The number of bits per second that can be transmitted in a given computer system.

Binaural. The ability to listen with both ears. Used in association with telephone headsets.

Blocked Calls. Calls that receive busy signals.

Boom. A stick-like device which places the microphone of a telephone headset in front of the user's mouth.

BPS—Bits Per Second. Refers to the speed of information transmission.

Broker's Hold. A telephone feature that allows a user to switch between two conversations without establishing a conference call.

Busy Out Device. A device that senses one line ringing in and automatically cancels out others with a busy signal.

Call Accounting. Generally refers to equipment that provides a record of calls placed by extension, time, date, number dialed and length of call.

Call Diverter. Redirects calls from one telephone number to another prearranged phone number (see Call Forwarding).

Call Forcing. Used in conjunction with headsets, it "forces" a waiting call onto an available agent as soon as that person has completed a previous call. The agent receives an audible tone burst that signals that no effort is necessary to receive this call.

Call Forwarding. A telephone feature that programs calls to be directed to an individual at another station or outside location without the caller having to dial the alternative number.

Call Management System. A machine which gives detailed information on telephone activity and cost.

Call Override. A telephone feature that allows stations to interrupt a call by another station connected to any third unit in the system.

Call Parking. By "placing" a call on hold or an imaginary extension, the call can be retrieved from any other phone within the system.

Call Restriction. The precise range of calling power given to employees. Can be designed so that certain phone users will only be permitted to make internal calls, and only selected personnel will be able to make long-distance calls (see programmable Toll Restriction).

Call Sequencer. Allows operators to make the decision in longest idle calls. Has basic management information reports. Also makes announcements to callers in overload situations.

Camp–On. Allows incoming calls to wait on a line until it is available, at which time the call goes through automatically.

CBX—Computerized Branch Exchange. See PBX for functions.

CCR—Communicator Call Report. Identifies each telephone communicator (or sales rep), calls that were handled, the date, the contact name and all information pertaining to the details of each call made during the shift.

CO—Central Office (Incoming Lines). Telephone company facility where subscribers' lines are joined to switching equipment for connecting other subscribers to each other, locally and long-distance.

CPU—Central Processing Unit. The main control unit of a switching or computer system.

DCE—Data Communications Equipment. Includes telecommunications devices such as modems and telephone lines within a basic data communication network.

DID—Direct Inward Dialing. A system in which a company buys a package of numbers, usually in lots of 100, and assigns individual users an access number of their own so they can call into the office and receive an outside trunk connected to the company (see DISA).

Direct–in Lines. If one department or employee receives the bulk of incoming calls, direct-in lines allow regular callers to reach the people they need without going through the central console, thus speeding call-handling and giving the attendant more time to extend courtesy to others.

DISA—Direct Inward System Access. A telephone feature which allows an individual who is away from the office to call into a special number at the office, dial an access code and receive an outside company trunk including WATS, Tie lines, etc. (see DID).

Display Telephones. Sometimes called smart phones—provide an English language display of what extensions calls are forwarded to and under what circumstances—no answers, busy signals, etc.

DMR—Detailed Message Recording. See DSMA.

DOV—Data Over Voice. A process by which the same wires are used for both telephones and computer terminals for simultaneous voice and data communications.

DSMA—Detailed Station Message Accounting. Specifies details of numbers called, listing the most often reached areas, etc. Can highlight system abuses and pinpoint or lead to optimum configurations.

DSS—Direct Station Selection. A telephone feature that provides single button access for in-use status of all stations and page zones.

DTE—Data Terminal Equipment. Includes the computer and terminal equipment.

DTMF—Dual Tone Multi–Frequency. Refers to push-button or touch-tone telephones.

800 Service. Inward WATS service offered by some common carriers that allows callers to call toll-free with the call recipient picking up the charge (see WATS).

Electronic Mail. The process of sending messages electronically from a computer terminal to a message printer located at an individual's desk, or a central point in the office or plant, thereby providing the recipient with hard copy communications.

Facsimile (Fax). A method of information transfer including typewritten or hand written letters, diagrams, drawings, etc., which occurs over telephone lines to remote locations for an exact hard copy of the duplicate at high transmission speeds. An electronic mail system.

FIFO—First-In-First-Out. See queue.

Follow-up System. Part of a software program that keeps track of calls that should be recycled into the outgoing program and rescheduled at a later time. Its purpose is to trap information and release it back to communicators at the appropriate time.

Fulfillment System. A software feature used for calls that require sending a fulfillment package to the prospect or purchaser. Its purpose is to produce the fulfillment package or lists for fulfillment operations, to ensure that the proper package is sent out. Very often a word processing system is used in meeting this requirement.

FX—Foreign Exchange Lines. Provides local telephone service from a central office which is outside the subscriber's switching area.

Hardware. Physical equipment excluding functional software properties, i.e., the housing cabinets.

Hold Recall. A telephone feature that alerts the user that a call has been on hold for longer than a preset period of time.

Host Computer. Main or central computer.

Hot Line. Any stations registered as hot lines can be reached without dialing.

Hybrid Key System. A telephone system which has attributes of both key telephone systems and PBXs. Usually means that incoming lines appear as key system lines and outgoing dialing arrangements are similar to a PBX, namely that one has to dial "9" to make an outside call. Hybrids can generally handle standard single line telephones as well as proprietary electronic instruments.

Inbound. Calls that come into a telemarketing center.

Intercom Callback Request. An electronic message can be left with someone else within the organization for someone who is out of the office or tied up on the phone. The internal caller's station number appears in the digital read-out display of the other person's phone automatically.

Interconnect Companies. Private telephone companies.

ISDN—Integrated Services Digital Network. Universal, digital network will be able to plug in not only telephone, but computers, word processors, and other office equipment.

Key Systems. A group of electronic telephone instruments commonly recognized by the rows or buttons located on the sets which are used to access all line services. They are mostly used by operations with 2 to 100 telephone sets (see Hybrid Key Systems).

KSU—Key Service Unit. The operational equipment vital for the functioning key systems. (Also referred to as Key System Unit.)

LAN—Local Area Network. Usually contained within one building (see Network).

LCD—Liquid Crystal Display. Shows status of real time calling activity or other functions of the system.

LCR—Least Cost Routing. Equipment automatically makes a decision for the user as to the most economical method of calling telephone numbers, routing outgoing calls via the most cost-effective lines available to the system, i.e., AT&T and other common carriers. (See OCC.)

LED—Long Lasting Light Emitting Diodes. Used in place of incandescent bulbs for display phones.

Line Capacity. The total number of in-house telephone lines that a switch can accommodate.

MERS—Most Economical Route Selection. See LCR.

Micro, Mini and Mainframe Computer Systems. Difficult to distinguish from one another in terms of levels of support. Currently, the main differentiating factors are cost, processing speeds, storage capabilities, number of terminals supported and microprocessing capabilities.

Microphone Mute Switch. A device that allows headset wearers to turn off the microphone so as not to be heard by the parties to whom they were speaking.

Modem. A device that converts computer generated digital signals into signals that appear wavelike or analog—or vice versa—to allow transmission over telephone lines.

Multiplexor. Allows one telephone line to be shared by several terminals. Also spelled multiplexer.

Mute Key. A telephone feature that allows the user to keep a party on-line without the party hearing what is transpiring.

Network. Usually refers to a basic telecommunications/data communications system which consists of a central computer, two modems, telephone line and a remote terminal.

Noise Cancelling. A feature of some telephone headsets which drastically reduces or eliminates background noise with the use of two microphones.

OCC—Other Common Carrier. Also called specialized or alternative common carriers. Companies offering long-distance telephone service in competition with AT&T.

Off-net. Meaning off the network. Commonly used in conjunction with other common carriers, referring to geographic areas not accommodated by a long-distance service company.

One Ring Dialer. Single line telephone instrument that automatically dials a predetermined telephone number when the receiver is lifted off the hook.

OTC—Operating Telephone Company. A user's local telephone company.

Outbound. Calls that are directed out of the telemarketing center.

Override Features. Allows designated stations to bypass and thus interrupt features such as busy line, automatic privacy.

PBX—Private Branch Exchange. A private phone switching system allowing communication within a business and between the business and the outside world. Calls are received at a centralized console for rerouting or can be designated to individuals. Modern PBXs are automated and called PABXs (Private Automated Branch Exchange). Sometimes they're called CBXs for Computerized Branch Exchange.

Pulse Only Telephone. Rotary dial telephones.

Queue. A function of an ACD which holds all inward bound calls in a line, in the order in which they arrive until the next available agent takes the first in line, moving the next call behind into the front position.

SMDR—Station Message Detail Recording. When used in conjunction with an ACD, will record and provide reports on traffic and station usage as well as telemarketer performance. Cuts down on unauthorized phone use by issuing a print-out that tells who in the organization called whom, at what time, how often, for how long and at what cost.

Software. The intelligent program within a system, such as a computer, that makes the system function.

Source Identification. An audible identification of where the next call an agent is receiving is originating from in terms of geographic location. Part of an ACD system.

Switched Telephone Lines. Identical to those used in the home. Provide dial-up service between devices in which only the time connected is billed.

Telecommunications. The transmission of audio information over a distance by electromagnetic means.

Telephone Record Control. A device used to record and/or monitor both sides of a telephone conversation based on on-hook or off-hook conditions.

Teleprinter. Equipment used to "electrically" transmit data from one point to another.

Toll Restriction. Allows for selection of which telephones will have the ability to access long-distance lines.

Trunk Capacity. The number of outgoing circuits connecting your site to the telephone company.

Trunk Queue. If no lines are available for an outside call, the call will be put in a queue and the caller's phone will automatically ring as soon as a line becomes available.

Turnkey. Designating a method of construction and assembly whereby the contractor assumes responsibility from the design through completion of a project or product.

UCD—Universal Call Distributor. A telephone device that puts telephone agents in a circular list with a pointer which indicates the next agent to receive a call, and automatically distributes that call.

User Friendliness. A term used to describe operational ease, convenience and comfort of otherwise technical or highly sophisticated equipment.

Voice Store-and-forward. Commonly known as voice mail where two-way audio correspondence is accomplished via the telephone and computer. Typically a human verbal message is left and converted for future use.

WATS—Wide Area Telecommunication Service. Potentially lower cost long-distance service. Allows calls to specified service areas in one direction only, incoming or outgoing, not both.

　　Ask questions. Once you are familiar with telecommunications terms, you can begin to have conversations with vendors and suppliers. Your part of these conversations generally should be questions because you need to gain as much information as possible in order to make a good decision.

　　One of the first questions you need to ask of yourself is

whether to buy or rent your telephone system. Usually businesses come out ahead when they buy rather than rent their phone systems. Compare the price of renting over a period of 10 years. Could you buy a system for that amount? If you could, how long would it meet your needs? Figure in depreciation for your phone equipment. Where do you break even—or do you come out ahead?

You'll also want to investigate the advantages of dealing with manufacturers and retailers. A retailer offers a wider selection of systems. A manufacturer can provide a guaranteed supply of equipment and parts as well as factory trained technicians to install and service the equipment. Both should offer a parts and service guarantee.

Just as a smart consumer goes shopping with a list, a telephone shopper should have a list of questions in hand . . . It should cover equipment, equipment features, and service.

Equipment—Phone systems must be flexible so expansion, relocation and modification are easy. The average user adds 20 to 30 percent phone capacity every five years. Can the system handle this?

Expansion will be possible if you can move up to the next system level by changing the central unit rather than changing each phone. You should be able to add features with software, which is less expensive than changing phone equipment. System wiring should provide compatibility with other equipment, (RS 232 is the computer industry standard), and the system should have more wiring than you initially need.

Not only will you need to expand the system, undoubtedly you will want to move phones within the office or perhaps to other locations. How easily can the phone system move—and how easily can it be reprogrammed? The software features of the system also should make it easy for you to expand or modify the phone system as your needs change. Can each phone be individually programmed? Can anyone accomplish the task, or will it require a special technician? How user-friendly are the system equipment and software?

System features are another decision point. How many features and which ones for whom? The most important function of the phone is its ability to make and receive calls. Other features, such as call forwarding, handsfree service or SMDR are directly proportional to the benefit and use you and your staff gain from them. Common sense and task analysis of your operation will help you distinguish essential features from technological toys.

Service may be the most important feature of your phone system. If the phone system isn't working, or isn't working properly, the telemarketing operation will be at a standstill.

Read all the fine print of the service contract. What's covered? How quickly will you receive service? A three-hour response time is the phone industry norm for emergencies in a standard business day. Normal service should be received within 24 hours or the next business day.

How easily can you diagnose what's wrong with the system? Can you program the phones or change call features without a service call? What training have the service technicians had? And will they have access to parts for your system?

The telephone is your most important sales tool. After asking all these questions, you will be able to sift through the information and select a system that will work for your operation.

The final test of your decision comes with installation. **Don't be impatient.** Prepare staff and customers for the installation of a new system. The phone system supplier should be able to help you prepare staff for the transition—it's never smooth.

Even telemarketers who are very happy with their phone systems after a month or two always report that the first days were rocky. Set up some practice calls before the system is activated to the outside. Let people practice not only the new technology but also the new vocabulary of their phone systems. By planning for the break-in period, confusion and frustration will be minimal; therefore, the impact on the customer at the other end of the phone system will quickly be productive and efficient.

The Telephone Bill

As you begin to plan a telemarketing operation, you should analyze the current telephone costs of your business, just as you analyze the current marketing and management strategies. A telephone audit will give you an information base that will allow you to look at alternative cost control to increase profitability.

DO:

• **Examine the components of your current phone bill.**

Basic service and equipment can amount to almost 30 percent of your total phone bill. It's important that you separate these and itemize the costs since this is the area of phone costs which can be most often controlled by management. Are the phone lines in use? Do they work? Is your phone equipment cost-effective for your operation? These are some of the questions your review should answer.

Local Message Unit Calls or MUs are calls that are charged a toll as opposed to unlimited flat-rate local service. Your calling pattern can have a dramatic effect on this phone bill component. It may make sense for you to subscribe to an Extended Area Service if you make frequent calls outside the radius of your local message unit. You will also need to look at the long-distance calls billed to your phone system. You'll need to compute the average cost per minute in order to compare long-distance rates with possible savings from Wide Area Telecommunication Service (WATS) lines, both inWATS or outWATS. If WATS is used properly, you can reduce your toll call expenses by 10 percent or more.

You will also want to explore the Specialized Common Carriers (or Other Common Carriers) that have their own circuits in competition with AT&T system lines. For some calling patterns, the SCCs provide cost reduction, for example credit card and operator assisted calls. A final component of your phone bill, other charges, may include things such as moves, installation fees, telegrams and directory advertising.

After you have reviewed each section, you should determine the percentage cost of each phone bill component. This will give you an idea of the component with the most potential for cost reduction and help you plan a course of action that will control telephone costs for maximum profitability.

Automating The Telemarketing Operation

The most important function of telemarketing communicators is closing the sale, yet they may spend a large portion of their time performing paperwork tasks or dialing numbers or waiting for a call response. The introduction of computer technology to the telemarketing operation may be one of the most productive innovations a telemarketing manager can make.

Telemarketing managers who have automated some or all of their telemarketing operations discover, almost immediately, a variety of benefits. Communicator productivity and morale increases; supervisors, relieved of paperwork, can really manage the telemarketing center staff; account executives make quicker and better decisions with more information at hand; and the net result is significantly better penetration of the market.

A management team considering, or already involved in telemarketing, is aware of the labor intensive nature of telemarketing and probably aware of the computer's ability to efficiently handle routine and repetitive tasks. The problem is how to successfully introduce the right automation option. How large must an operation be to justify the investment? Do you have to be a computer whiz to put together a system that works? How large is the investment in hardware—and what about software systems? Some simple guidelines can provide a basis for launching the telemarketing team into the computer revolution.

DO:

- **Make the psychological commitment to investigate a new technology.**
- **Consult the needs of the telemarketing team.**
- **Select software—then look for the supporting hardware.**

DON'T:

- **Try to remedy a telemarketing problem with an automation solution.**

The process of introducing automation into the telemarketing center begins with evaluation. Is the telemarketing operation as successful as it could be given current conditions? Are communicators properly trained? Are they working with effective scripts? Is sales volume erratic, perhaps because advertising and promotion are not integrated with telemarketing sales? **Don't try to remedy telemarketing problems with an automation solution.** Automation will only support certain kinds of activity. It will not replace good management or creative thinking. If the telemarketing center is operating at an efficient and productive level, automated support will increase success.

Make the psychological commitment to investigate a new

technology on the basis of your telemarketing operation and its needs. The manager who decides to automate the telemarketing center will discover that the process requires a new look at the way work is done. First analyze the current activity of the telemarketing center in order to determine which individual (and labor-intensive) tasks can be efficiently accomplished by a computer.

In an outbound telemarketing operation, as much as 70 percent of the communicators' time may be allocated to functions other than the sales conversation. A large outbound telemarketing operation in the Northeast introduced a computer that automatically dials prospects' phone numbers on a priority based system that integrates call-backs into the calling sequence at the appropriate time. The result: communicators can now speak with 20 percent more people per hour.

Another area that lends itself to computer support is follow-up. Communicators working with an interactive system can initiate orders, send confirming letters or designate call-back times by striking a few keys. The results of their calls are also immediately available to supervisors who can monitor productivity and spot developing trends concerning a particular script, product or calling region.

Even when a system isn't completely interactive, automation can support increased efficiency. A bank on the west coast decided to set up a telemarketing unit to solicit customers for loans and other financial products at some of its local branches. The unit staff spent the last day-and-a-half of the month sorting through telephone logs to compile a monthly report. By instituting a batch system which processed data through the bank's central computer, the manager captured the reporting time for additional sales activity.

Analyze each telemarketing task to determine the level of automated support useful in a specific operation. One telemarketing center's need for on-line interaction may be another's need for manual notes and batch system follow-up.

Consult the needs of the telemarketing team; the final product will be more end user effective and more readily accepted. One of the by-products of a careful review of the telemarketing operation is the involvement of the potential end user in establishing the requirements of an automated system. By including the communicators and supervisory staff in the task analysis, the telemarketing manager encourages subsequent participation.

Automation will necessitate change—a situation that can be threatening if the groundwork for implementation isn't carefully laid. If telemarketing staff feel a system is being imposed on them, they may be resentful or anxious, inferring that managment has judged their performance ineffective. They will respond enthusiastically to the system, however, if they feel that their experience and suggestions have been considered.

Once the in-house review has been accomplished, it's time to go shopping for a system. **Select software—then look for the supporting hardware.** Software is the "thinking" part of the automated system and its programmed instructions must meet the requirements of the telemarketing center as they have been identified by the management team.

Depending on the needs of a particular telemarketing center, a manager might look for a data base manager, a telemarketing system, a sales management system or a system that integrates or can be customized to include all three. It's important to continue the search until the right software is found: Impatient managers who think they can change the organization to suit the software court disaster.

Telemarketing software increasingly reflects the lesson that was learned in the personal computer market: Consumers want a machine that is easy to use and understand—they don't want to become computer programmers. Therefore, it's not only reasonable, but essential for the computer novice to conduct the software search as thoroughly as possible.

Get referrals of users who are working with systems in situations that are similar to your telemarketing center. Visit the site, perhaps involving the telemarketing staff to evaluate the system in use.

Look for a strong guarantee from the software publisher if you are buying from a mail order outlet.

Will you need to customize the software program? Make sure you understand the costs involved and whether the publisher will guarantee that subsequent updates to the system will work with your customization.

Look at the documentation. Spend some time reading the manual—is it intelligible to a first-time computer user?

What is the level of after sale support? If you dial the "customer information" number, do you receive help or a constant busy signal?

Telemarketing managers need to exercise the same kind of intelligent analysis when they're ready to purchase the computer hardware to support the software. The process of comparing technology, systems, and vendors may seem exhausting but the knowledge base it generates is critical for the computer education of the telemarketing manager.

By selecting the software first, the search for the computer is somewhat delineated because not all software is compatible with all hardware. Even so, there will be an array of options which initially may seem overwhelming. However, common sense purchasing rules still apply.

Look for a brand that has an established reputation. Talk with people who are using systems and get a feel for hands-on operation.

Consider potential needs as well as current requirements. Inevitably, familiarity with a computer system opens up a range of modifications and enhancements. A common mistake is to buy a system that fits the present perfectly—look for one that can accommodate the future.

Stay within your budget. Purchase price isn't the only consideration because system maintenance, system changes or expansions can exceed the costs of initial acquisition and installation.

Don't assume that a rock-bottom price is the best investment—it may be a sign of impending obsolescence.

Select a dealer that is helpful throughout your decision making process and who will provide after sale support. The transition to an automated operation will be less difficult if you can rely on professional assistance in the early stages.

When the automated system is carefully selected to meet the requirements of the telemarketing center, its impact will be immediate and dramatic. Supervisors are able to follow communicator activity rather than processing reports. Communicators are more productive and view their roles as more professional as they direct fulfillment tasks through the computer. Ultimately, the entire operation provides better customer service which, in turn, yields higher profits.

Data Support

Data support for a telemarketing operation is the basic building block of a system that responds efficiently to changing markets and strategies. Although office automation, which introduces computer technology into the data support equation, has had an explosive effect on telemarketing, many telemarketing centers have "manual systems" that are responsive to a company's needs. Whether data support is automated or manual, the guidelines for systems development are similar.

The telemarketing planner can develop a system which will have an impact on the entire marketing data base of an organization by keeping in mind three basic ideas.

DO:

• **Determine basic information needs.**
• **Understand the basic framework and functions of data support as it applies to telemarketing.**

DON'T:

• **Let technology set the pace.**

Determine basic information needs. The telemarketing planner should answer several questions in order to identify the basic information needs the data system should meet. What are the functions it will support? What specific data and information must be captured and managed? What is the volume of that data and its sources? What systems or areas in the organization will interact with the telemarketing data system?

For some firms, the answers to these questions may suggest that a manual system will be responsive to needs at least up to a certain volume level or given a certain kind of product.

A computer services firm on the west coast "naturally" looked at a completely interactive, computerized data system as a way to support its planned telemarketing center. Since it already had computer hardware, questions focused on issues related to software support. The firm particularly looked at the nature of its product and the most effective sales strategy. Its highly specialized computer service carries a price tag which ranges from $10,000 to $350,000. In-house people are specially trained to qualify 10 or 20 serious prospects from thousands of advertising responses and to communicate in technical language in order to sell the product to engineers.

Although it had wanted an on-line, completely automated data system for the new telemarketing center, the company found that customized off-the-shelf software was cost-prohibitive—even when using hardware already in place. Instead, it developed a system in which information is captured manually and then entered into a data base.

As a business in the computer industry, this firm was a step ahead when it came to identifying information needs, particularly with respect to automation. For the telemarketing planner without this background, it's important to review industry terminology before beginning to analyze the organization's needs.

Data Processing: a way to manipulate data to generate information. Data processing functions include recording, classifying, sorting, summarizing, calculating, disseminating and storing. A computer automates these functions and reduces the amount of time people must spend on these tasks.

Micro, Mini and Mainframe Computer Systems: the hardware and accompanying software which processes data.

Data Base: the collection of data which supports the information needs of a specific group of users. If a company wants to develop both inbound and outbound telemarketing functions, four primary data bases will be necessary:

1. *Customer Data Base:* contains information about current and past customers and their purchases.
2. *Prospect Data Base:* a list of potential customers or potential customers who have been contacted but haven't made a purchase.
3. *Product Data Base:* contains data identifying products, pricing, and costs as well as performance and possibly budgetary information.
4. *Media Data Base:* tracks methods or campaigns used to reach a customer or potential customer, including the data to evaluate the results of these efforts.

Understand the basic framework and functions of data support as it applies to telemarketing. Data bases are developed and updated through processing systems, both automated and manual, which generate three levels of information support—planning, control, and functional. Systems begin at the functional level and move through successive modifications to control and planning levels.

At the functional support level, telemarketers can capture data about their marketplace from the marketplace itself. The

Communicator Call Report (CCR) is the primary document at this level. The CCR must be designed to incorporate data elements which are specific to the company's market, products, and requirements. However, CCRs typically include four sections:

1. *Customer or prospect identification and demographic data.* This is the time to get the facts straight, i.e., company name, address, contacts and their titles and telephone numbers, and to capture information which will smooth the next sales call: time zone location of office; best calling times; type of business; number of employees; date of last purchase; products purchased, or credit classification.
2. *Fact finding data regarding contact.* This section can function like a market survey, e.g., source of media contact, product(s) of interest, product application or frequency of use.
3. *Disposition data.* Contained here are notes about the continuing sales process including customer ranking and potential value, disposition (sales lead, fulfillment package, inquiry, sale), follow-up date or time.
4. *Order entry data.* These elements depend on a company's specific order entry requirements including purchase order number, product code, quantity, shipping requirements and delivery dates.

In addition to data collection, data processing at the functional level supports a variety of operational activities which contribute to efficient telemarketing. The components of each system may be more or less automated depending on a firm's needs, but the processing channels, or systems, should allow for rapid communication between the organization's departments in order to meet company goals.

List management system: manages customer and prospect lists. Compares in-house lists and purchased lists, purges duplicates and selects names for direct mail promotion and outbound telemarketing.

Lead fulfillment system: identifies qualified leads and generates reports to the field sales force. Will also track leads and monitor follow-up and reporting.

Follow-up system: keeps track of calls that should be forwarded to the outgoing program and rescheduled.

Order entry system: if a call terminates with a sale, the system directly processes the order or holds information until it can be entered in a batch.

Reporting systems: generate reports, update data bases and detail the activities of the telemarketing center. Reports may deal with the performance of the telecommunications system itself, the performance of individual communicators or of the communicator group. On weekly or monthly basis, other reports may analyze the effect of the telemarketing operation on the various data bases.

The data systems at the functional level must capture enough historical data to identify trends. As projections and forecasting systems are developed from the primary source data, the control level measures costs and performance against a standard, budget, or goal.

At this level, the effectiveness of the system depends on the ability of the management team to identify priorities within the company's environment. User-oriented reporting capability becomes very important at this stage to ensure that ad hoc information requests can be quickly met.

At the highest level of the data support system, planning and analysis introduces data from outside the organization. Comparisons with industry standards, analysis of economic factors, new product development or introduction to markets and long-range forecasting require sophisticated techniques. Some firms turn to outside organizations at this stage of their data systems evolution.

The evolution of the data system should keep pace with the ability of the management team to assimilate techniques and project new needs. It's important to maintain this perspective in spite of the lure of technological enhancements.

Don't let technology set the pace. If telemarketing planners first identify the needs of the organization and institute systems that meet those needs, the data processing system can be successfully integrated into the overall organization. The result will be a system that is not only cost-effective, but also accepted as an effective way to enhance productivity.

Chapter 7

Telemarketing Techniques

Companies that have instituted successful telemarketing operations know that the process isn't a simple shift in marketing methodology, but rather a change to direct, targeted marketing through telecommunications. Telemarketers face many challenges in adopting this new methodology but they gain a set of tools which can enhance the productivity of the entire sales effort.

Script preparation, list management and sales verification are three basic functions that support successful telemarketing operations. In addition, telemarketers must test, test, test—at every point of the process to ensure an effective script, an efficient fulfillment effort, or quality leads.

Sometimes it makes sense for a company to look to a telemarketing service bureau to perform these functions, either as a supplement to an in-house telemarketing center or as the primary telemarketing operation. As a supplement, the service bureau can help meet seasonal demands, take on a specific project which otherwise would have required an unjustifiable investment in equipment, or serve as a continuing source of sales activity if an equipment or power failure disrupts in-house activity.

Telemarketing service bureaus can do everything from planning campaigns to sending out fulfillment packages. Whether you do some or all of your telemarketing through a service bureau, it's important that you understand the basic telemarketing techniques. The next sections will describe guidelines for script preparation, sales verification and list management, as well as some tips for TSRs.

Scripts

Is a script always necessary in a telemarketing environment? Are there some circumstances that require absolute and precise repetition of questions? How easily can a script be written? How much sales technique is required to structure it?

Scripts can vary from outlines to word-for-word CRT (or manual) scripts. If your presentation is a simple consumer or business-to-business transaction, you can generally use a well-designed script, written on paper (although today's software technology allows for replies to objections to be presented instantly to TSRs which greatly enhances the chances for selling success). More complex scripts, usually written for business-to-business applications, often allow more telephone representative flexibility.

While word-for-word scripting may require technically sophisticated equipment for interactive delivery, a script that prompts key points and phrases requires more sophisticated sales representative technique. Your choice for sales presentations can fall anywhere between these extremes—and still be successful—if you remember these points.

DO:

• **Prepare a script that conveys the message in an orderly flow of information and persuasion.**

DON'T:

• **Allow the telephone sales reps to "wing it."**

The next section looks at scripting for outbound consumer and business operations. While there are considerations which differ, two are important in dealing with both audiences.

To **present the message in an orderly flow** when using a highly structured script, you must have a skilled copywriter who has a good ear for conversation. If you don't have a good writer on staff, hire one.

If your situation requires communication flexibility, you still must provide some structure; **don't let sales reps wing it.** They will not be productive if they wander through a presentation willy-nilly.

Outbound Telemarketing Scripts

Script—the term conjures up images of plays or movies, stars and directors. Telemarketers often use analogies from drama and the stage to describe the role of telephone sales reps and the function of the scripts they use. Just as a good action can sometimes compensate for a poorly written script, a telemarketing superstar may be able to close a sale in spite of a badly designed presentation. But what about the majority of reps—how do you ensure that they have the most effective sales tools at their disposal?

DO:

- **Begin by analyzing your product and your sales goals.**
- **Incorporate proven sales techniques into the presentation.**
- **Test and practice until enthusiasm can be heard in every line.**

DON'T:

- **Adapt the copy from a direct mail offering.**

By now it must be apparent that there are no short cuts in developing a successful telemarketing operation. It's absolutely essential that you know what your goals are at every level of the operation. At the script level, you must answer some basic questions which will help to define the message of your script.

Begin by analyzing your product and your sales goals.
What makes my offer better than those that are similar? Who are
my prospective customers and what are they like? Have they had
contact with my organization or a similar one? What happened?
Can we quickly establish credibility? What are the turn-on and
turn-off points of my offer?

In large telemarketing environments, the marketing manager and the telemarketing manager will define the script's sales
objectives. They may involve consultants, script testers, scriptwriters, technicians and telephone supervisors and representatives. In less formal situations, the sales manager, or even
company owner, may determine the objectives of the script. In
both situations, however, **incorporate proven sales techniques
into the presentation.** What will work for your TSRs and your
product? Remember that on the plus side, the telephone call has
the singular distinction of bypassing all forms of prejudice—what
matters is what you have to say. On the other hand, when you call
people at home, they will assume that you want the conversation to
end at the expense of their pocketbooks and wallets.

Since the objective of the call is to make a sale, you'll want to
structure the presentation toward a strong closing. The *alternative
closing* assumes that the sale is made. After stating the product
information and consumer benefits, the telephone rep says "Which
will be better for you, A or B?" This conveys a positive attitude and
encourages borderline respondents to make a positive decision.

The *drop closing* lets you work around the natural inclina-
tion for people to say "no" the first time they're asked to make a
decision. Determine the largest logical quantity the consumer
might buy. Ask for the purchase. When the automatic "no" comes
forth, drop to the next logical amount. By planning for this natural
behavior, you can take advantage of the live, direct sale conversation that occurs during a telemarketing presentation.

Once the sales strategies are defined, scriptwriting is in
order. The person who is in charge of scriptwriting and message

design should have copywriting credentials and should understand the characteristics essential for effective telemarketing communication. This may be a time to work with an outside consultant if no one on the current staff has this background.

The most frequent mistake inexperienced scriptwriters make is to forget they are creating a conversation, not an advertising piece. **Don't adapt the copy from a direct mail offering.** Textbook English has no place in a sales conversation on the phone. As one script consultant has said, the minute the script begins to sound as if it could be written underneath a picture, stuffed in an envelope and dropped in a mailbox, do yourself a favor and toss it into the nearest wastebasket.

Use a tape recorder to develop a natural, conversational flow for the sales presentation. **Test and practice** until enthusiasm animates every line. You want to duplicate, as much as possible, the persuasive and agreeable dialogue your most successful telephone sales rep has with each customer.

These guidelines are generally applicable to both consumer and business-to-business outbound telemarketing. Product information, which is often more complex in the business-to-business situation, introduces another planning element into script preparation.

Scripting For Business Telemarketing

Although there are many similarities between outbound telemarketing to consumers and businesses, one of the key differences is the emphasis on developing and maintaining a long-term account in business. Month after month, you want to sell computer products or business stationery to the same company. Therefore, the telemarketer is your representative in the marketplace. The script he or she uses is a reflection of you and your company. How can script development enhance your image and help you obtain a greater share of your market?

DO:

• **Analyze the company's marketing requirements and sales environment.**
• **Determine the target market and the target prospect.**
• **Bring together tested script and sales techniques.**
• **Test, test, test.**

DON'T:

• **Let your expectations exceed your capabilities.**

Identify your goals. Experienced telemarketers again and again ask, "How will you know you've succeeded if you don't know where you're going?" **Analyze the company's marketing requirements and sales environment.** Telemarketing integration with the overall marketing effort is essential. Whether you design the script to generate qualified leads for a field sales force, to verify field sales and try for sales upgrade, or to maintain accounts, the telemarketing goals must be firmly in place.

The goal setting stage is a time for realism as well as enthusiasm. You may be delighted that you have your field sales team and your telemarketers ready to work together to launch a new product or you may be excited about launching your first-ever telemarketing campaign. **Don't let your expectations exceed your capabilities.** An effective business-to-business script lasts no longer than three to five minutes and typically contains only five to eight questions. You must focus on a specific goal and refrain from trying to get one script to accomplish all of your sales goals in one campaign.

Once you have established your sales goal, **determine the target market and the target prospect.** Your sales team, whether field or telemarketing, can help you profile your typical "buyer." Use your team's perceptions to create a profile that will help you develop an effectively scripted conversation. Consider general attitudes toward being sold, educational level, salary and position status, background and general characteristics of the individuals. Is your target prospect an engineer, a CEO, a purchasing agent, an executive assistant, or a financial analyst? The answers to these questions may determine not only how you will prepare a script, but who will deliver it!

Writing a script may be more of an art than a science and its creative requirements are those of a skilled craftsperson. If you don't have skilled staff writers who understand the telemarketing medium, you may want to consider outside help with this aspect of your operation. In working with your scriptwriter (or if you've taken on this task yourself), here are some tested guidelines to keep in mind:

1. *Write in concise and specific conversational English.*
2. *Keep in mind the vocabulary of the product.* If you're selling to engineers, know that your sales rep will need a lot of product training to be able to speak in engineering terms.

Never launch a full campaign until you **test, test, test.** Any script will contain rough spots that will only emerge during on-line interviewing. Set up a test on a sample population. Monitor the telephone reps and listen to responses, terminations and respondent reactions. Is the script fulfilling its purpose—achieving your goal? Are you generating leads or closing sales? Are you creating interest in your product? Rewrite and test as many times as necessary until you can answer the questions affirmatively.

Tips For TSRs

The way you organize the telemarketing center will contribute to performance, but there are techniques that will be handy for individual TSRs.

DO:

- **Plan the presentation.**
- **Know the product or service—and know the competition's.**
- **Qualify the decision maker.**
- **Catch buying signals.**
- **Project sincerity.**
- **Convey enthusiasm and confidence.**
- **Be courteous.**

DON'T:

- **Forget to close the sale.**

A large telemarketing organization says that 75 percent of its salespersons quit after their first rejection but 63 percent of all sales are made after the fifth rejection. Unless a TSR maintains control of the conversation in the face of the initial rejection, valuable sales will be lost.

To maintain control, **plan the presentation.** A plan allows the TSR to keep the focus on the product or service, creating a context in which there is a potential benefit for the customer. Many telemarketing operations insist that the TSRs use a script, although some business-to-business applications use call guides which provide a general framework for the presentation. All successful telemarketers, however, develop some kind of plan because it frees the mind to revise strategy as the customer responds to the sales call.

TSRs establish credibility when they demonstrate that they **know the product or service—and know the competition's.** Many of the objections a customer raises will be based on comparison with similar products. TSRs can build customer confidence and acceptance by analyzing the product from different perspectives, for example, technical specifications, ROI and service benefits. This lets TSRs vary the sales presentation to accommodate customers who have different roles in their respective companies. The key is to speak to decision makers in their own terms. Thus, it's important to **qualify the decision maker.**

Be prepared to encounter people whose job is to screen the decision maker's calls. Be prepared—but don't settle for "no." A courteous approach to dealing with a call screener is to enlist that person's support in reaching the decision maker. But if the screener can't be moved, and the call is important, some TSRs will call after (or before) standard office hours. Support staff may have left and sometimes key people will answer the phone.

Once the key person is on the phone, deliver the presentation, but listen carefully and **catch buying signals.** Novices may be so enamored of the presentation (or so nervous) they miss a buying signal. Recognize that the presentation is a dialogue and stop talking long enough to hear a signal that the customer is ready to buy.

Project sincerity and convey enthusiasm and confidence. If you have confidence in the quality of the presentation and confidence in the quality of the product, you can project sincerity and enthusiasm. Putting a smile in your voice, even when you've given the same presentation many times throughout the day, is essential. Project an image of the customer and try to talk as if you were face to face.

Be courteous. You're representing your company, and most importantly, yourself. If you're confident about the benefits that the customer will get from your product, you can be assertive without being discourteous.

Finally, **don't forget to go for the sale.** As soon as you sense that the customer has reached a decision to buy, confirm the order quickly and with thanks. TSRs who continue a presentation beyond the point of decision often talk themselves out of a sale. "One of the most important lessons I learned," according to a young telemarketer for a small gift wholesaler in South Carolina, "was to ask for the sale. My company expects that I will be relaxed with my customers and that's good to a point. But after some time on the phone, I realized that I had to take control. Now I still keep things low-key, joke and chat as we become familiar, but I make sure that I go for the closing. If I don't ask, I won't have the order."

Sales Verification

The sales verification process can be an invaluable internal control tool because it will help minimize unwarranted clerical and fulfillment expenses. If you're using a telemarketing service agency for part or all of your telemarketing operation, you should understand what sales verification can mean for the overall cost effectiveness of your telemarketing effort.

During the course of a typical telemarketing day, hundreds of prospects are called—and many say yes to your offer or product. The telephone sales rep who closes that call, however, will not have a contract or a bill of sale. The TSR will only have verbal cues and commitments. These cues may be distorted by the telephone connection or noise in the phone room. The TSR may also be functioning under a high quota demand. You should anticipate errors and misunderstood or misrepresented sales.

As you talk with telemarketing service companies, explore their approaches to sales verification and their documentation to their clients. There are three common techniques that are used, but they can be modified in a variety of ways.

Continuous Monitoring. Managers silently monitor TSR calls throughout the daily calling periods. Supervisors randomly listen to one TSR at a time, checking for courteous attitudes, continuous dialing, recording of proper information and proper script usage.

Call Back Verification. A selection of each TSR's daily work is called again to check for correct recording of information, attitude toward call recipients and quality of sales or interviews.

Tape Recording. Recording of all or part of each call. Some agencies record only the closing to verify agreement terms. Surveys or interviews are often completely recorded after securing permission of the call recipient.

Some service vendors emphasize front-end factors, feeling that professionally structured telemarketing campaigns will ensure strong back-end results. These vendors suggest that a service-oriented attitude, where the client's image is of primary importance, will reduce the pressure for a sale.

In-house telemarketing managers often emphasize a similar point. They note that their telephone reps respond favorably to encouragement and discussion in regular feedback meetings while they may be resentful about the supervisor listening to their conversations.

Individual applications will determine the kind of verification that should be built into your telemarketing process. The results of verification justify this extra effort; you'll increase the efficiency of your operation and enhance your relations with your customers.

List Selection And Technology

Telemarketing is frequently defined as targeted sales. The best product in the world will remain on the shelf if you can't find the individual who will buy it. Lists are at the heart of the direct marketing industry. Whether you develop your own list or use one of the 60,000 consumer and business lists now available, you must define your market and determine how you can reach it.

DO:

- **Draw as broad a market outline as possible.**
- **Call list brokers for advice.**
- **Test.**

DON'T:

• **Confuse a cheaper list price with a bargain.**

The first step in developing a prospect list is relatively simple. Use your own customer base as a starting point. What do you know about your customers? What other groups are likely to have interest in your product or service? In other words, **draw as broad a market outline as possible.**

With this information in hand, you're ready to **call list brokers for advice.** Brokers can review your assumptions and the results of any tests you've conducted. They can identify the best group of lists for the early phase of your campaign and they can help you plan an evolutionary market schedule.

Computer technology has increased the viability of lists for telemarketing use. If you don't consult a list broker, you should take into account the advances which can provide the most cost-effective lists in the long run. For example, licensed firms compile most business and household telephone directories as soon as they are published. These firms make the names and numbers available to computer service bureaus. In turn, the bureaus match client mailing lists against the telephone files which results in a large savings over traditional directory assistance methods.

However much or little you rely on purchased lists to generate your prospective customer base, test your decisions at every step of campaign development. Since each list will produce a different response, segment the lists and analyze them separately. You also should consider analyzing the variables within each list in order to increase your net return.

You may have a pretty good understanding of your market and customer characteristics—but you may not be tapping the best way to reach them. Your investment in testing and in list selection will pay off. **Don't confuse a cheaper list price with a bargain.**

The ultimate cost of a lead is measured by whether or not it generates a sale. Even on a small scale, the cost of looking up and appending telephone numbers without benefit of computer matching will make it impossible for your telemarketing center to show a profit.

Chapter 8

Additional Telemarketing Applications

Lead Qualification

Lead qualification is an especially effective telemarketing application because it identifies prospects who possess the three essentials of a potential sale—the need, authority, and resources to acquire a product or service. Lead qualification combines market research and advance sales techniques to sort out lukewarm prospects from really hot sales leads.

You should set up a lead qualification program within the context of the company's overall marketing plan. In this way, lead qualification will support other sales activities because it will be defined within the established sales goals of the company.

How do you establish the lead qualification program? What are the guidelines a new telemarketer should keep in mind?

DO:

• **Develop a customer profile.**
• **Generate a prospect pool likely to develop into leads.**
• **Institute a follow-up program which will transform a hot lead into a completed sale.**

DON'T:

• **Be insensitive to the potential conflict between the field sales and telemarketing staffs.**

As with any telemarketing application, the implementation of a lead qualification program requires planning, planning, planning. A first step is to **develop a customer profile** based on an analysis of the characteristics of your current customers. The TSRs who conduct the lead qualification campaign will be screening against these characteristics which may include type and size of business, buying frequency and quantity purchase of similar products.

This preliminary profile can help you identify the sources that will **generate a prospect pool likely to develop into leads.** The two sources typically used for lead generation are media advertising (radio, TV, print or direct mail) and lists purchased from brokers.

Before picking up the phone to call these prospects, however, the telemarketing center must prepare a script or outline to qualify or disqualify a customer as quickly as possible. Does the lead match your customer profile? What is the prospect's current situation; for example, is he satisfied with his current supplier? Does the prospect look for price, quality, delivery in selecting a supplier?

Salespeople will also be helped by information about the prospect's awareness of your company, product or service. At this point, the lead qualification call becomes an opportunity to lay the groundwork for the future sale by providing advance information to the prospect.

TSRs can also facilitate field sales by probing for information about the decision making procedure at the company. Are bids necessary or can the purchaser requisition a product? Who is involved in a purchasing decision and at what level? The answers to these questions will really prepare the salesperson for getting down to business.

Lead qualification will be only a market research function unless you ensure a rapid follow-up process. **Institute a follow-up program which will transform a hot lead into a completed sale.** You must anticipate the fulfillment requirements your lead qualification program will produce. Can you get the leads to field salespeople immediately? Will they be prepared to call the customer? If your procedure requires a mail follow-up after the initial phone contact, will your mail room be prepared to handle the material?

Perhaps the most critical factor in the follow-up process is the degree to which the sales and telemarketing staffs see themselves as a team. **Don't be insensitive to the potential conflict between the field sales and telemarketing staffs.** The ultimate success of your sales program depends on their cooperation and could be ruined by their conflict.

In some situations, an uneasy truce may exist which prevents the telemarketing center from yielding maximum benefits to the company. The telemarketing manager for a medical instrumentation firm has set up a productive system for lead qualification, yet the telemarketing center's effectiveness depends on the willingness of individual salespeople to follow up the leads.

"This is a traditional, 'press-the-flesh' company and some die-hard salesmen feel that telemarketing is going to infringe on their territories. We channel our information through the marketing and communications departments, which immediately take advantage of the research benefits of our leads. But we could be doing more.

"Top management is finally taking a good look at the benefits of telemarketing. Our management team is also press-the-flesh oriented—it's a strategy that has made us No. 1 in our field. However, it's clear that a salesman can't do everything in today's competitive market. And management is beginning to realize that the salesman who is going to sell $25,000–$100,000 instrumentation should have the benefit of every support, including telemarketing. I'm optimistic that we'll soon be able to convince the sales staff that we are comfortable with telemarketing's supportive role in our company. We aren't trying to take over their territories."

Converting Customer Service Into Sales

Many businesses have found that telemarketing can convert their already established customer service departments into profit centers. Whether consciously or unconsciously, people who make a decision to buy a product want that decision affirmed. This is a pool of people who are likely to become loyal customers if their needs for good service are met.

Telemarketing, however, requires sales techniques, not the skills for which customer service people are normally hired. To convert an existing service department into a productive tele-marketing customer service center, you must carefully consider both attitudinal and technical issues.

DO:

• **Consider the impact of change on your current employees.**
• **Be prepared to identify and train for new, sales-related goals.**

DON'T:

• **Overlook the possibility of using outside consultants to implement your transition.**

Successful telemarketing managers consistently talk about the importance of treating their employees like valued human beings. The conversion of a customer service staff into a sales staff is another instance where it's absolutely essential for managers to take the time to consider the impact of a change on the people who will implement it.

Consider the impact of change on your current employees. The strength of your current customer service staff is also its weakness—it's established. Your people know the company and your clients, yet their original job description probably did not mention sales. They never represented themselves as having sales skills when they were hired for their current jobs. If you attempt to change, in a fairly radical way, their job requirements, and more importantly, their perception of the skills needed to do the new job, you should be prepared for confusion, anxiety and a drop in productivity as morale takes a plunge.

As a manager, you must be alert to the reactions of your staff. Who is excited about a new challenge? Who is reluctant but willing to go along with the decision? Who is going to quit? You must be ready to help the customer service staff reach a new definition of its role within the company. Make it clear that they are not being asked to pitch a product or service. Rather they will be offering solutions to problems or concerns.

If you can work with staff to accept this definition, you may be able to overcome the negative stereotype that many of them may have about sales. If they have negative images about salespeople, they will set themselves up for failure in their new role by projecting their own prejudice onto the customers. "I hate talking to salesmen—why would anyone want to talk to me? I'm selling."

However, if this customer representative realizes that the product or service that's being offered may meet a need or remedy a problem for the client, that same person will feel much more comfortable in this new role, in which sales becomes an extension of service.

Be prepared to identify new sales-related goals and develop a training program to achieve them. One of the foundations of the transition will be to work from the knowledge base of the current staff. Training can then be targeted toward specific concerns or skill areas, which may include:

Identifying Sales Opportunities.

Understanding the Sales Process.

Mastering the Service Sell, (i.e., offering a product as the solution to a problem).

Overcoming Objections.

Translating Product Features into Benefits.

Developing Probing and Listening Skills.

Using Closing Techniques.

Controlling the Sales Interaction with Each Customer.

Since the emotional climate may be somewhat charged during this time (after all, you're changing the expectations by which people earn their livelihoods), **don't overlook the possibility of using outside consultants** to implement your transition. Either a training team from another area of the company or consultants from outside will be less threatening because they will be viewed as being objective. This may be particularly important during the information gathering phase which should precede the goal setting and training phases.

While many of the skills and techniques that make TSRs effective are also useful for people fulfilling a customer service representative (CSR) role, there is, at the very least, a difference in emphasis. An efficient manner, a sense of moving the conversation along are still important. However, the customer has initiated the service call. The need which prompted the call must first be met or the transaction will fail. Thus, it's very important that the CSR have a high degree of product knowledge and be able to respond to the specific complaint appropriately, before moving into a cross-sell mode.

Customer Service
For Business-To-Business Markets

Customer service, important certainly in the consumer market, may be even more important in the business-to-business market. Rather than complain, many business people who are unhappy with a product or service "get even." They may limit purchases or stop buying from a company completely. Even worse, they may complain to others in their business community about the problems they have had.

Your telemarketing center could come to the rescue of your business by making it easy for a customer to get satisfaction when there is a problem.

DO:

• **Integrate customer service functions to provide a comprehensive response system for your business customers.**

DON'T:

• **Go into an aggressive service mode without planning carefully.**

Integrate the customer service function; it can be an asset which will increase valuable product loyalty and word of mouth customer support. At least seven separate functions can be set up to meet the needs of your customers. They include:

1. *Soliciting a call at a point of product use likely to result in a problem.*
2. *Giving advice on your general product area or the specific use of your product.*

3. *Turning a complaint call into a sales call.*
4. *Identifying information which will lead to new or improved product.*
5. *Providing actual product service over the phone.*
6. *Handling potential claims immediately.*
7. *Capturing data for quality assurance.*

Each of these functions requires proper training for the telephone representative, who must be aware of some subtle differences in customer expectation. For example, if a customer calls for some general product advice it may be better to provide the advice and defer any solicitation of sales for another time. On the other hand, a customer who calls with a complaint—and gets it resolved—may be a likely candidate for a sale of accessory items or another product.

As helpful as these areas can be to your overall sales effort, **don't go into an aggressive service mode unless you have planned carefully** to avoid setting up expectations before your delivery system is in place. Each of the functions will need its own shakedown period in order for you to assess the efficiency and effectiveness of your operation. You need to provide special training for your customer service reps on each aspect of the service they may need to provide. You may even need to have people with specialized skills available for certain kinds of calls, for example product service.

You should also make sure that your representatives will be compensated for the level of customer satisfaction they generate. This customer service mode is not simply a numbers game, it's a way to ensure a loyal and positive customer base. In a marketplace that offers the buyer a lot of options, a business can differentiate itself from the competition by providing comprehensive customer service through telemarketing.

Tips For Business-To-Business

Establish rapport with receptionists and secretaries. Be polite, friendly and warm, each and every call. The people who screen the telephone calls hold the key to the door of your decision maker.

Listen to your prospect. Your potential customer knows more than you do about his business or service. You're going to sell your product as a way to meet his needs—so find out what they are.

Keep a positive attitude in the face of rejection. You aren't the target when the prospect says no. Recall your past success and remember how effective you can be.

Don't miss a chance to cross-sell or upgrade existing customers. Let your customer service department become an extension of your sales effort.

Don't overstay your welcome. If it is clear that you are not going to be able to sell your product on this occasion, end the call quickly and gracefully. You may want to call another day and you don't want your prospect to remember you as the boor who couldn't understand the word "no."

Chapter 9

The Last Word: Ethics

If you have worked your way through all of the learning, planning, strategizing and implementation outlined in this guide, you are seriously committed to telemarketing practices so it is likely that you also will be committed to telemarketing principles.

DO:

- **Identify yourself and your reason for calling.**
- **Cultivate good telephone manners.**
- **Promote professional practices in public forums.**

DON'T:

- **Lie or make false claims about your service or your product.**
- **Violate the privacy of people who choose to "unlist" themselves from public directories.**
- **Disturb consumers during unreasonably early or late hours.**

These principles may seem to be such obviously good business practice, you wonder that they need to be published. The undisputed but sad fact is that many individuals and businesses have seized on the remarkable efficiency of telemarketing to make a remarkably quick buck—and then they move on, to another locale or another product, leaving hundreds of consumers calling for legislative action.

One of the things that most irritates consumers is the "machine call." The message from consumers (and "machine" phone calls are largely a consumer phenomenon) seems clear—if people are going to be called, they want some other person to have taken the trouble to call them.

On the other hand, "machines," i.e., automatic dialing recorded message players are too cost-effective to be ignored. The problem isn't as much the machines as the way they are used—and that's within the control of people.

If you are going to conduct business-to-business telemarketing, it's important that you look at your telemarketing center as an extension of your marketing organization. Whether you conduct the operation in-house, or use an outside agency, you should not take the cheapest or quickest road to profits if it will compromise ethical selling practices in any way. You do not want your company image to be associated with "junk" calls.

There are several steps that you can take to ensure that your telemarketing organization works in a professional and ethical manner.

DO:

• **Make sure the message from the top is that ethical practice is a priority.**
• **Hire the right people.**
• **Use your training program to instill your values.**

The message from the top should be clear: You place a priority on taste, integrity and customer reaction. You can reinforce this by developing an efficient administrative organization. For example, consumer lists should be coordinated so prospects receive only one call from your company. Scripts must be fair and TSRs should understand that they are not to promise a prospect more than the offer you have determined.

Hire the right people. During an interview, the candidate has a chance to evaluate you. Make it clear what your standards and expectations are. Let candidates who are daunted by your standards screen themselves from consideration. You should also check references. This is the time to separate assertive sales talent from unethical operators.

Your training program plays an important role in shaping the conduct of your telemarketing operation. Does the TSR know how to gracefully end a conversation—even if the prospect says no? Does the TSR understand that enthusiasm for a sale doesn't excuse suggesting more of a benefit than you are offering?

Finally, how do you reinforce your TSRs for proper implementation and maintenance of standards? Do you respond quickly to customer complaints? Are you prepared to terminate a rep who doesn't meet standards? Prompt action is sometimes necessary to guard the reputation of your company.

By making a decision to become involved in telemarketing, you are joining an industry that is constantly expanding the limits imposed by today's highly competitive market. Telemarketing is the best way to identify a customer, i.e., someone who will buy the product more than once, in contrast to a "sale," which implies a one-time only encounter. The measure of your success will be not simply short-term profits, but the long-term economic health of your business. You will be able to take advantage of a powerful tool which is no longer viewed as just another way to sell, but rather is viewed more and more as the only way to sell.

Telemarketing® Magazine

Cumulative Subject Index

This index was compiled by subject and includes article title, month and year of publication, and beginning page number for each article that has appeared in Telemarketing® magazine since its inception in 1982. Back issues can be obtained by calling Telemarketing® magazine, 800-243-6002, or 203-852-6800. Specific articles can be found under one or several of the following subject categories:

Applications

Button Down Telemarketing On Wall Street, September 1985, 15.

Call Accounting For Financial Services, August 1984, 48.

Controlling Word Of Mouth Through Group Telemarketing, June 1984, 32.

Effective Telemarketing Implementation For The Wholesale-Distributor, November 1983, 22.

Healthcare Telemarketing Comes Of Age, October 1983, 42.

Improving Cash Flow With Tele-Collections, June 1984, 20.

Insurance Telemarketing: An Old Tool With New Meaning, August 1985, 44.

Is There A "Tele" In The Future Of Bank Marketing?, February 1985, 49.

Outbound Telemarketing Strategies For Selling Small Business & Telecommunications Systems, February 1984, 8.

Signature's Success Shows That Insurance & Telemarketing Do Mix, August 1985, 54.

Telecommunications Equipment Sales: A Revolution In Progress, April 1984, 32.

Telemarketing And The Petrochemical Industry, February 1983, 50.

Telemarketing Boosts Trade Show Effectiveness, Nov./Dec. 1982, 54.

Telemarketing In The Insurance Industry, October 1984, 12.

Telemarketing, The Productivity Tool For The Insurance Industry, June/July 1982, 18.

The Bank That Banked On Telemarketing, October 1984, 16.

The Personnel Profile For Insurance Telemarketers, August 1985, 50.

The Soaring Success Of Telemarketing For Aircraft Prospects, July 1984, 34.

Using Telemarketing To Sell Telecommunications Services, April 1983, 16.

What It Takes To Succeed In High-Tech Telemarketing, October 1985, 50.

Automatic Call Distributors
ACDs: Painting The True Performance Picture, December 1985, 32.

Automatic Call Distributors In A Telemarketing Environment, February 1983, 14.

Dialing For Dollars With Automatic Call Distributors, June/July 1982, 7.

How Call Accounting Trims Telemarketing Costs, March 1985, 28.

Telemarketing Call Management, June 1983, 32.

Telephone Call Accounting: Management Tool For The 80's, January 1984, 26.

Telephone Cost Accounting For Operations Management, June 1984, 30.

The Call Accounting Marketplace—Roundup, March 1983, 32.

The PC-Based Call Accounting Alternative, March 1985, 38.

Vendor Vs. In-House Call Detail Recording, March 1985, 30.

What Every Buyer Should Consider Before Investing In A Call Accounting System, December 1984, 24.

Case Studies
Barnes & Noble: A Success Story Of Textbooks And Telemarketing, Nov./Dec. 1982, 16.

Call Accounting For Financial Services, August 1984, 48.

Computerized Telemarketing Helps Keep Air India Flying High, February 1983, 55.

Cons Are Pros At Inbound Telemarketing, January 1985, 32.

Grolier & SNET Team Up To Develop $40 Million Telemarketing Sales, June/July 1982, 13.

How A Small Company Achieved Great Success Through Effective Telemarketing, June/July 1982, 25.

How Automation Has Improved Our Telemarketing Services, April 1985, 53.

How Automation Turned A Telemarketing Service Bureau Into A $10M Organization, November 1984, 16.

Live Aid: Telemarketing's Finest Hours—How It All Came Together, September 1985, 38.

Cellular Mobile Communications
A Layperson's Primer On The Cellular Telephone Industry, October 1984, 24.

Cellular Mobile Communications And Its Impact On Metro Areas, October 1984, 20.

Cellular's Future Shock, August 1985, 30.

Mobile Data Link Takes Telemarketing Into The Field, August 1985, 34.

Welcome To The Wonderful World of Cellular Mobile Communications, December 1984, 38.

Common Carriers
How The Telephone Companies Handle Telemarketing Demands, June/July 1982, 11.

Simple Steps To Long-Distance Selection, December 1985, 42.

The Creation Of An Industry, August 1984, 24.

The New Generation Of Long-Distance Services, July 1983, 45.

Compensation
Comparative Compensation Practices In The Telemarketing Industry, July 1983, 38.

Compensation For Telemarketing Sales Reps And Supervisors, February 1983, 52.

Telemarketing Compensation Practices '85, August 1985, 60.

The Complete Compensation Update—1984, August 1984, 32.

Computerized Data Management
Before You Buy That Computer System...Basic Computer Terminology, December 1983, 6.

Computer Based Message Systems For The Telemarketing Manager, February 1984, 28.

Computerized Management Of Sales Information Leads To Better Decision Making, September 1984, 56.

CRT/Video Display Terminals: Behind The Screens—Industry Report, September 1983, 33.

Data Support For Telemarketing, Sept./Oct. 1982, 46.

Selecting The Data Network That's Right For You, March 1984, 8.

Telemarketing And The Microcomputer, Sept./Oct. 1982, 36.

The Basic Components Of Network Planning And Development, July 1984, 20.

Computerized Telemarketing
Automated Telemarketing: Out Of The Fog, July 1985, 64.

Automation Peaks Productivity, April 1985, 50.

Automation—A Telemarketing Manager's Dream, December 1985, 18.

Computer Supported Telemarketing, July 1983, 6.

Computerized Telemarketing Helps Keep Air India Flying High, February 1983, 55.

Computerized Telemarketing—More Than Just Sitting TSRs at CRTs, April 1985, 28.

How Automation Has Improved Our Telemarketing Services, April 1985, 53.

How Automation Turned A Telemarketing Service Bureau Into A $10M Organization, November 1984, 16.

Rethinking And Retooling For The Telecomputer, June 1983, 20.

Taking The Plunge: How To Computerize Your Telemarketing Department In Four Easy Steps, December 1983, 12.

Ten Situations To Avoid As You Convert From Manual To Computerized Telemarketing, November 1984, 8.

The Manager's Guide To Automating The Outbound Phone Room, May 1984, 12.

The New Language Of Telemarketing And Associated Techniques, July 1983, 42.

The Next Generation Of Telemarketing Systems, August 1985, 38.

Fundraising
The Strategy Of Fundraising By Phone, October 1983, 40.

Headsets
A Comparative Look At Telephone Headsets, November 1983, 30.

Commodity Brokers Give Headsets A Blue Chip Rating, November 1985, 34.

Headsets Are Valuable Property To The Real Estate Industry, November 1985, 36.

Headsets—Phone Fatigue Busters—Roundup, November 1985, 30.

New Developments In Headset Design Improve Efficiency, February 1983, 24.

The Expanded Role Of The Telephone Headset, November 1984, 24.

The Telemarketing® Roundup Of Headset Suppliers, November 1984, 28.

The Telephone Headset: Ideal Complement To Telemarketing's Primary Tool, Sept./Oct. 1982, 14.

Inbound Telemarketing
Advertising For Information, June 1983, 8.

Cons Are Pros At Inbound Telemarketing, January 1985, 32.

Displaying 800 Numbers For Best Results, June 1983, 18.

How An 800 Number Can Expand Your Market Power & Turn Service Into Profits, December 1984, 30.

How To Use Telemarketing For Inquiry Handling And Lead Fulfillment, Nov./Dec. 1982, 8.

Interactive Voice Telemarketing—An Inbound Marketing Tool, June 1985, 20.

International Marketing Goes Toll-Free, September 1983, 52.

Putting An End To Telefraud, January 1984, 18.

The Impact of the 800 Number on Consumers' Telephone Shopping Behavior, December 1984, 34.

The Most Effective Way To Market With 800 Numbers, July 1985, 36.

TV Advertising And Telemarketing: An Outrageous Opinion, August 1983, 42.

Lead Generation/Qualification
How To Acquire Telemarketing Sales Leads. . .& Put Them To Work, October 1984, 30.

Lead Qualification: The Proven Path To Reducing Sales Costs While Improving Results, May 1984, 36.

Telemarketing—The Difference Between Cold Leads & Hot Prospects, September 1983, 43.

The Qualifying Call, October 1985, 94.

Lists
List Selection For Greater Market Penetration, March 1984, 32.

List Technology: A Telemarketing Asset, May 1985, 40.

Outbound Telemarketing—Maximizing Results With List Segmentation And Data Base Management, December 1985, 56.

Local Area Networks (LANS)
Microwave Radio: A New Alternative In Data/Voice Communications, February 1984, 6.

Telemarketing And The Local Area Network, May 1985, 36.

The Communications Manager's Guide To Determining A Network Approach, July 1984, 22.

Long-Distance Resellers
Examining Resellers Of Long-Distance Services—How They Work, August 1984, 30.

The Creation Of An Industry, August 1984, 24.

The History And Emergence Of Long-Distance Resellers, August 1984, 20.

Management
Budgeting For A New Telemarketing Center, August 1985, 72.

Voice-Data PABX Meets Office Automation Needs, December 1983, 32.

Overview, Telecommunications

From Hieroglyphics To Today's Communications Satellites, May 1984, 23.

Glossary Of Terms, December 1983, 35.

Long-Term Outlook For The Telephone And Telegraph Industries, November 1985, 42.

Opportunities For U.S. Telecommunications Exports To Japan, September 1985, 70.

Telecommunications Industry Outlook '85, Part I, May 1985, 16.

Telecommunications Industry Outlook '85, Part II, July 1985, 54.

Telecommunications' Journey Through 1990, December 1984, 44.

The Potential For Telemarketing And Telecommunications In The Far East, July 1984, 9.

The Rising Role Of Shared Tenant Services, December 1985, 46.

Overview, Telemarketing

A Practical Approach To Telemarketing, Sept./Oct. 1982, 8.

Determining Telemarketing Profitability, October 1983, 8.

Does Telemarketing Really Work?, January 1984, 37.

Heart Transplants, Airplanes, Baseball, Apple Pie And Telemarketing, February 1984, 22.

Inside Telemarketing: Revealing Probe Into The Growth Of The Industry, August 1983, 6.

Lawmakers Focus On Key Telemarketing Issues, June 1985, 12.

Perspectives On Future Telemarketing Trends, November 1985, 58.

Preparation Is The Key To Telemarketing Profitability, July 1983, 16.

Telemarketing At A Glance: A Blueprint To Increasing Business Productivity, Sept./Oct. 1982, 57.

Telemarketing's Believe It Or Not!, March 1984, 44.

Telemarketing: Is It For You?, June/July 1982, 33.

The ABC's Of In-House Telemarketing, July 1983, 20.

The Biggest And Most Repetitive Mistakes Telemarketers Make, November 1984, 20.

The Potential For Telemarketing And Telecommunications In The Far East, July 1984, 9.

The Telemarketing Industry: Where We Are, Where We're Going, July 1985, 22.

The Telemarketing Program—How To Get Started, October 1985, 36.

The Transition From Field Sales To Telemarketing: Avoiding The Pitfalls, August 1984, 40.

When Not To Use Telemarketing, January 1984, 39.

Paging Systems
The New Role Of Electronic Paging In The Delivery Of Information, May 1985, 30.

The Potential Of Nationwide Alpha-Numeric Display Paging, May 1984, 28.

PBX, PABX, Key Systems
Considerations In Implementing A PBX System, Sept./Oct. 1982, 18.

How To Buy A PBX, November 1983, 14.

How To Determine When To Upgrade Or Purchase A New PBX, September 1985, 52.

Inbound/Outbound Telemarketing Is Enhanced By A PBX/ACD, September 1984, 60.

Key Features Of Key/PBX Systems—Roundup, April 1984, 14.

Key Systems Versus PBX—Changes To Date, February 1985, 14.

Key Systems—Key Manufacturers—Roundup, February 1985, 22.

Tour Of Telemarketers' Telecommunications Systems—Survey, February 1985, 32

What To Look For In Telecommunication Workstations, October 1983, 26.

Private Line Service
Cutting Telecommunications Costs With Private Line Service, April 1984, 16.

Private Line Service: An Answer To The Multiple-Choice Network Test, April 1984, 10.

Private Network Communications In Perspective, April 1985, 22.

Recruiting
Become A Telemarketing Hiring Specialist With The 27 Point Hiring System, February 1985, 44.

Determining The Predictive Success Of The TSR Applicant, May 1985, 34.

How To Evaluate A Telemarketing Managerial Candidate, October 1983, 13.

How To Hire Top-Notch Telemarketers Through Selective Screening, February 1985, 46.

How To Recruit And Select Quality Telemarketers, November 1984, 36.

Looking For Mr. Goodvoice: The Crux Of Manpower Planning, December 1983, 22.

People Power: How To Hire The Best People For Your Telemarketing Center, Nov./Dec. 1982, 47.

Put On Your Telemarketing Recruiter's Hat—It's Unique To All Others, February 1985, 40.

Recruitment, Training & Supervision: Tactical Tools For Success In Telemarketing, June/July 1982, 35.

Scripting
How To Conduct Product Research For Script Development, July 1984, 25.

Staff Management

An Overlooked Management Basic—Dealing With Unproductive Employees, March 1984, 38.

Career Path Planning—It Takes Two, June 1984, 36.

Coordinating Inside & Outside Sales Forces: A Compensation Approach For Greater Productivity, February 1983, 34.

High Turnover? Several Alternatives, September 1983, 49.

How to Handle TSR Burnout In Account Management Centers, December 1984, 14.

How To Tally TSR Talent, April 1984, 44.

Is Turnover A Serious Problem?, April 1983, 54.

Molding A TSR Into An Effective Manager, November 1985, 50.

Multiple Roles Increase Telemarketers' Productivity, September 1984, 66.

People: Still A Critical Factor In Your Telemarketing Setup, August 1984, 44.

Strategies For Dealing With Problem Employees, November 1985, 46.

Switching Systems

Digital Switching—The Key To The Wired World, August 1984, 16.

How To Enhance Telemarketing With Telephone Switching Systems, August 1984, 38.

Least Cost Routing In The Telemarketing Environment, March 1985, 43.

Lifting The Mystique Of Telecommunications Switching, March 1985, 40.

The Unique Switching Requirements Of Telemarketing Companies, Nov./Dec. 1982, 34.

Viewing Digital Communications From The User's Perspective, August 1984, 12.

Techniques For Telemarketing

Checklist For Success In Telemarketing, October 1985, 40.

Tele-In-Focus (Monthly Column)

Appendices

Appendix I

Checklist For Selecting A Telemarketing Service Vendor

Company Background And Experience
__ Length of time in business
__ Financial strength
__ Services provided
__ Experience with similar programs
__ Past & current clients
__ Commitment to telemarketing
__ Ability to integrate telemarketing into total marketing program

Management
__ Management team's background & experience
__ Personality of key personnel
__ Business philosophy of management
__ Activity within the industry (organizations, seminars, books, etc.)
__ Number of TSRs, full time or part-time
__ Type & size of support staff
__ Size & organization of client services staff
__ Lead time for changing lines & equipment
__ Willingness to accommodate individual needs

Cost And Pricing
__ Fee structure for setup & script development (fixed, hourly, no charge)
__ Training charges

Cost And Pricing continued
__ Telemarketing charges (hourly, per call, per inquiry)
__ Clerical & administrative costs (fixed, hourly)
__ Reporting: What is standard, what is extra
__ Fulfillment (invoiced per item or hourly)

Operations
__ Line capacity/types of phone lines available
__ Flexibility
__ TSR quality
__ Employee practices & policies
__ TSR training programs
__ Ratio & physical setup of supervisor to TSRs
__ Controls & monitoring procedures
__ Adherence to schedules
__ Timeliness of reporting to clients
__ Type of telecommunications equipment used
__ Type of telemarketing software
__ Availability of support services
　　__ Financial
　　__ Data processing
　　__ Fulfillment
　　__ Delivery
　　__ Recorded message capability
__ Length of time systems & equipment have been in operation

Miscellaneous
__ Location of telemarketing center

*From *How to Select a Telemarketing Service Vendor*, by Richard Herzog, Telemarketing®, July 1985, p. 14.

Appendix II

The 27-Point Hiring System

The 27-Point Hiring System is designed so you can, in a brief telephone interview, systematically rate your candidate in the following areas: voice quality, rapport and telemarketing experience.

To begin the interview you will want to ask a few basic questions such as the ones listed below to take control of the conversation and gain information about the candidate.

1. Why are you interested in the job?
2. Have you ever worked on the telephone before? Why did you like it? What didn't you like about it?
3. What do you consider to be your strongest points in terms of telemarketing?
4. How do you feel you react to/handle pressure?
5. How many calls can you make in an hour?

If time permits and the applicant has indicated previous telephone sales experience, you may wish to ask the candidate to give you a presentation used in the past.

Now that the conversation has begun, you can rate your candidate accordingly:

Voice Quality

Within the 27-point total on the hiring profile, 10 are connected to voice quality. Voice quality includes diction and articulation, voice volume, rate of speech and tone, and can be determined in the following manner.

• *Diction And Articulation:* You may score 0,1,2, or 3 points, with 0 the low score, and 3 for really excellent clarity, expression and choice of words. As you are listening, ask yourself, "Can I understand this person without difficulty?" If candidates are hard to understand because they have a pronounced accent or slur their words, they may not be appropriate for telephone work. Also, their choice of words may influence their rating in this area. For example, you would give a high score to a candidate who projects a professional quality or image through the use of the language.

• *Voice Volume:* For this category score 1 if the voice volume is appropriate or 0 if not. Considering you sometimes have a bad phone connection, volume should be moderate. You don't want to consider someone whose voice is so soft you have to strain to hear him, or on the other end of the scale, so loud that you are forced to take your ear off the receiver.

• *Rate Of Speech:* The best way to determine whether an individual's rate of speech is "normal" is to compare it to your own. The normal rate of speech is about 150 words a minute. If there is a significant, noticeable difference that is distracting, again give the appropriate rating of 0 or 1.

• *Tone:* This is a critical category for which you can award up to five points on the profile. The tone of a person's voice can tell you a lot about the person—give you a mental picture of what he or she is like. Candidates who can interest you, the listener, with the tone of their voice or who can project an enthusiastic, business-like tone would naturally score higher than candidates whose tones vary, or who simply project a disinterested or otherwise unacceptable tone.

Rapport

Establishing rapport is another important factor in the development of any phone conversation and thus you can assign up to 10 points for this area. Although a great deal of rapport is built on the quality of the voice, there are additional questions you may wish to consider when rating an applicant in this area.

122

For instance, has the person attempted to instill trust and build your confidence? If trying to sell you something, would you believe what was said? And finally, have the candidates asked relevant questions that will help them make their own decision about the job?

Telemarketing Experience

The rating scale in this area is between 1 and 5 points. Generally, assign 1 point for up to 6 months of telemarketing experience, 2 points for 6 to 12 months, and 5 points for over 1 year of experience. Asking the candidate to give you specific information about previous job responsibilities may also help you determine a score.

Finally, other sales experience may add an additional 2 points to the scale.

Tallying The Score

At the conclusion of the interview, the points can be tallied. As a rule of thumb, 17 is a good applicant, and 20 points is excellent. For those who fall somewhere in the middle, say between 15 and 17, consider having them read a script before making a final determination.

If you find your results varying a great deal from this general rule, you may want to consider revising the stringency of your scoring.

Scoring the areas discussed can be changed to suit your particular hiring needs. For instance, you might want to give added weight to past job experience and length of time spent on the job depending on whether you are hiring full- or part-time people or on the level of difficulty of the sales call objective. You might want to be more stringent in your scoring of rapport building and voice quality if you expect your staff to make cold calls.

*From *Become A Telemarketing Hiring Specialist with the 27-Point Hiring System*, by Joel Linchitz & Leslie Kerby, Telemarketing®, February 1985, p. 44.

Appendix III

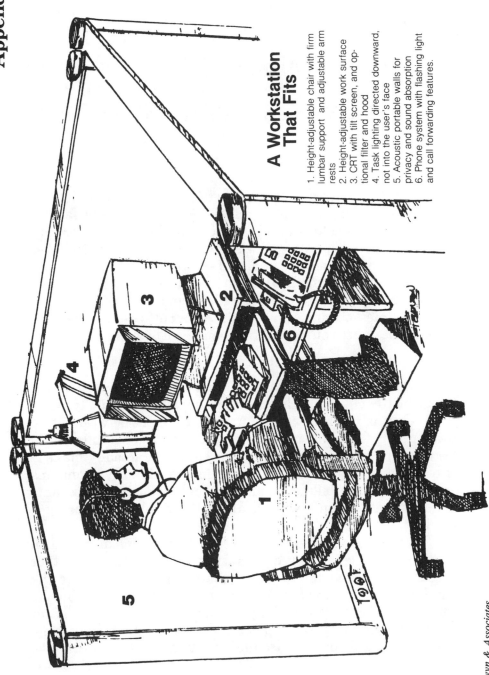

A Workstation That Fits

1. Height-adjustable chair with firm lumbar support and adjustable arm rests
2. Height-adjustable work surface
3. CRT with tilt screen, and optional filter and hood
4. Task lighting directed downward, not into the user's face
5. Acoustic portable walls for privacy and sound absorption
6. Phone system with flashing light and call forwarding features.

Courtesy of Selwyn & Associates

Appendix IV

Analyzing Your Long-Distance Phone Bill

There are three factors to use in selecting a long-distance carrier: cost, features and quality. To compare these factors, however, you need to obtain the following information for each long-distance company you wish to consider: (a) a complete description of the service and its features, (b) a complete and current rate chart for both intra and interstate calls, and (c) copies of relevant tariffs, if the company files them. The 800 number of the companies offering equal access to your office or home will be listed in the notice you receive from your local telephone company.

Cost

For most people, it is the "bottom line" that is most important; which company is "cheapest" for the calls you actually make.

Cost is not the rate per minute for calls between cities. Rather, it is the total cost for using a service for a full month. Getting the rates per minute for the calls you actually make is only the beginning of the process, not the end. Monthly minimums or service charges, billing increments, prompt payment discounts and volume discounts will all affect the final cost of using a service.

You must analyze your present telephone bill and create a standard sample bill to use in making comparisons with other long-distance vendors. To create the sample bill, average the number of calls you make in a typical month. Then, determine the patterns in your normal calling and have your sample bill reflect those patterns. Important patterns include time of day (day, evening or night), place called and duration of call. For example, if you find that 10 percent of your calls are daytime calls to Chicago, the 10 percent of your sample bill calls should be the same. Make sure your sample bill includes the average total number of minutes of your monthly calling. This information is needed to calculate a volume discount.

Once you have created your sample/composite bill, calculate the cost of each call. You'll need to know the rate per minute for the specific call and the billing increment. Different companies bill for calls by the minute, by the half-minute and by the tenth of a minute. Obviously, the tenth of the minute increment is more precise and can make a substantial difference in cost if you make a large number of short duration calls.

Getting the information to make this calculation is not always simple. Not every company has a rate chart which shows rates for different mileage bands. If not, you'll have to determine the distance to each location you call. The mileage is determined from the point of the local office (area code and first three digits) from where the call is made to the local office (area code and first three digits) of the place called. Without computer assistance, use standard mileage or map distances, which in most cases will be adequate.

Once you get the rate information, you need to know how a company calculates its volume discounts. Some companies discount total use, others discount time-of-day use. You also need to take the billing increment into consideration. This is a challenge if you have used AT&T which bills by the minute; you don't have the details to know when shorter billing increments would make a difference. A hint: Subtract 30 seconds from each of your calls. This will automatically permit factoring billing increment.

Once you calculate the total cost of using a service for your sample/composite bill, you are ready to compare different features.

Features

Travel Feature—Generally, it is the travel feature that is considered most important. That is, how easy and inexpensive is it to use a long-distance service while away from home and office.

Account Codes—This service is perhaps most important to many businesses and could be of particular importance to telemarketers. Most carriers offer a service that permits calls to be identified to specific accounts.

Information Service—Most long-distance companies provide access to information operators. The 555-1212 number is universal and it connects calls coming into a local exchange to local information operators. The operators are employees of the local telephone company. Long-distance companies are billed for this service on a per-call basis. In turn, they add their cost and bill you, the consumer, for each call made. Different companies have different policies.

Quality

Compare the quality of the sound as well as the overall quality of service. Ask these questions:

- How easy is it to contact the company when you have a problem? (One test would be to call a company during peak, daytime hours and see if the phone is answered quickly.)
- How informed are the service people?
- Can you readily get credit for wrong numbers?

The main concern still continues to be the quality of the sound and the irritating "echo." The main differences in quality will then depend on the means of transmission utilized by the carriers and the design of their networks.

It is generally agreed that the following means of transmission are of the noted quality:

> Fiber Optic—The Best
> Coaxial Cable—Second
> Microwave—Third
> Satellite—Worst

Your Choice

Having spent the hours necessary to acquire the facts on cost, features and quality, you are ready to make a choice. Perhaps the most important lesson here is that you need not use only a single long-distance company. The best decision may well be to use several companies or services for different calls.

It is likely that one long-distance service is best for calls to one city, while another is better for calls to another city. This is when your ability to pre-subscribe to different long-distance companies on different lines might be convenient.

It is also important to maintain flexibility and to keep on top of changing rates and services. If you don't, you may find the company you have chosen is no longer competitive. Assign an employee to study and follow trends in telecommunication services. Companies of all sizes have done this for years with postage rates and services. Clearly, it is now time to take this step with telecommunications equipment and services. Once monthly costs approach $500 or more, WATS-type services should be considered. Further, if your firm has advanced equipment such as PBX (Private Branch Exchange), it may be possible to utilize "least cost routing" features. This is a built-in computerized routing of calls over the least cost available long-distance services.

There is no substitute for expertise and knowledge to assure that your long-distance costs are minimized.

*From *Simple Steps to Long-Distance Selection*, by Samuel A. Simon, Telemarketing®, December 1985, p. 42.

Appendix V

Telemarketing Scripts You Can Adopt

A Sample Lead Qualification Script *(Business-to-Business)*

Identification
"This is Jane Doe calling for Jones Financial Corporation. May I please speak with Mr. Smith?"

or

(if no name)
"May I please speak with your Chief Financial Officer, and who would that be, please?"

Secretary asks "What is this in reference to?"
(literature sent)
"We recently sent him some literature describing our financial services and I'm calling to follow up on that."

or

(current customer)
"Since you're currently leasing equipment with us, we're calling to better understand your future plans to acquire equipment. And I'd need to speak with Mr. Smith about this. Is he available?"

or

"We're contacting major accounting firms in your area to introduce you to our financial services. And I would need to speak with Mr. Smith. Is he available?" (Copy designed to get past the secretary should be vague, but sound important enough that she really has to put you through.)

Introduction once you reach desired contact
"Good morning, Mr. Smith. This is Jane Doe calling for Jones

Financial Corporation. In case you're not aware, we are a full service financial company servicing many accounting firms like yours. To better understand our market and your needs, I'd just like to take about two minutes of your time to discuss your plans to acquire and finance equipment in the future. Do you have a moment?" (A question or pause here should allow you to involve the contact and also determine if this is a convenient time or if you should call back. It's wise to position the call at this point as a fact finding mission in case the contact is not qualified).

Qualify
"Thank you, Mr. Smith. First may I just ask if you have plans to acquire a major piece of equipment within the next year?" Yes -continue. No - terminate call as Not Qualified ("Well, in that case, I won't take up any more of your time...")

Determine time frame (or other relevant criteria)
"And when would you expect to make that acquisition? Would you say... Within 2 months? 3 - 6 months? 6 - 12 months? More than 1 year from now?" If it's between 2 and 12 months, continue; otherwise terminate call as Not Qualified.

Gather other relevant criteria
"What type of equipment are you planning to acquire?
- *Computer (Mainframe)*
- *Copier*
- *Personal Computer*
- *Typewriter*
- *Other*
And what is the approximate cost of the equipment? Would you say...
- *Under $1000*
- *$1000 - $5000*
- *$5000 - $10,000*
- *$10,000 - $50,000*

- *$50,000 - $100,000*
- *Over $100,000 . . ."*

(You can prioritize based on this criteria, if appropriate.)

"And are you planning to lease the equipment?" Yes - go to Pitch A. No - go to Pitch B.

Pitch A (Plans to lease)
"Since you're planning to lease, you know the many advantages leasing offers. What I'd like to do is have our representative contact you so you can compare our leasing package with the program you have in mind. Which would be a better time for him to see you, next Wednesday or Thursday?"

Pitch B (Not planning to lease)
"Although you're not currently planning to lease, you may want to explore the many advantages leasing offers, such as improved cash flow and increased tax deductions. I'd like to have our representative, Jim Smith, contact you to discuss this in more detail. OK?" (The pitch should reflect the person's situation and information previously supplied. Sell them on why, given their situation and frame of mind, they should consider your proposal. Speak directly to their needs.)

General Hesitant (responds to "I'm just not interested" or "I don't think so")
"Well Mr. Smith, you're under no obligation. We'd simply like to give you this opportunity to compare our services with your current arrangement. Given your upcoming acquisition plans, we may be able to help you improve your cash flow. When is a convenient time for our rep to contact you?" (Responses to objections should emphasize an additional benefit and have a different close.)

Satisfied With Current Method
"I can understand that, Mr. Smith, but with our competitive rates

and flexible financing options, we may be able to offer you more alternatives worth considering. Let me have our representative discuss this with you in more detail, OK?"

We Always Pay Cash
"Mr. Smith you may want to consider the many tax advantages of a lease. Leasing reduces your tax liability by counting payments as expenses. Our representative can explain this in more detail. Which would be a better day for him to contact you, Tuesday or Wednesday?"

There is always the request for literature. This can be treated a number of ways.

If Literature Has Previously Been Sent
"We have already sent literature, Mr. Smith. Speaking with a representative is really the best way to have your specific questions addressed. Let me have our rep, Jim Smith, contact you on Tuesday. OK?"

No Literature Sent
"I'd be happy to send you literature, Mr. Smith, but our representative can provide you with more detailed information. Let me have him contact you, OK?" (The positive close to a lead script should allow for confirmed day & time for the appointment, the ability to schedule a time further out, if appropriate, and a quick and polite end to the call...)

"Fine then, our representative, Jim Smith, will see you 10 a.m. on Thursday, the 19th. Thank you for your time. I'm glad we could be of help to you. Have a good day. Goodbye."

A Sample Sales Script

Identify Self
"This is Jane Doe calling for ABC Equipment. May I please speak with Joe Jones?"

What is this in reference to
"We're contacting Mr. Jones regarding the ABC copier he recently purchased. Is he available?"

Introduction once you reach desired contact
"Good afternoon, Mr. Jones. As a recent purchaser of an ABC copier, would you be interested in an economical way to protect your investment? (Pause) I'm glad to hear that. That's why we're offering a low cost service agreement on your ABC copier. Let me tell you more about it..." (This is your opportunity to involve the prospect by use of a positive question, and position yourself.)

Pitch
"As you're probably aware, service calls now cost $50 for the 1st hour and $45 for each additional hour. And that doesn't include parts and travel time. So, should your copier need even a small repair, that could add up to a lot of money...

What we're offering is a one-year agreement that would include all parts and labor as well as travel time. And you'd get one-day service on the equipment.

For you, the cost would be only $150 a year, or just $12.50 a month. That's a lot less than the cost of a one-hour service call. So let me protect your investment with a 1986 service contract, OK Mr. Jones?"

Objections And Responses

Too Expensive
"Mr. Jones, I can understand how you feel, but remember that having the machine break down without this service protection can end up costing you a lot more. And you can always cancel the agreement if you find it's not working for you. So let me sign you up for 1986, so you'll be covered. OK?"

Our Machine Never Breaks Down
"I'm certainly glad to hear that. And I can see that you've had the copier since August of 1984. You know, after a while the machine parts can break down from lack of proper maintenance. And it can end up costing you a lot of money without this agreement. So, let me take care of this for you, Mr. Jones, so you'll have protection for the next year. OK?"

Sales Script: Magazine Renewal
"Ms. Jones, I'm calling today as a courtesy, to let you know that your subscription to ABC Magazine is due for renewal. And, as a preferred customer, you're now eligible for a special two-year renewal rate. You'll receive 104 weekly issues of ABC for just 50 cents a copy. That's a 50% savings off the newsstand price...

And what's more, each year you'll receive our 3 special Buyer's Guide issues, all at no additional charge. I'd like to just verify your mailing address so I can guarantee you these special savings. OK?" (If they're not interested, go to the drop down offer.)

Drop Down Offer
"Well, Ms. Jones, you may want to consider subscribing for one year. You'll receive one year of ABC for just $35 - a savings of $5 off the regular subscription price. And you'd still receive all of the special issues free of charge. So may I put you down for our one-year subscription or would you prefer the supersavings of our two-year rate?"

*From *Telemarketing Scripts You Can Adopt*, by Katherine Cavaliere, Telemarketing®, October 1985, p. 85.

Appendix VI

Direct Marketing Association
Guidelines For Telephone Marketing

Prompt Disclosure
Article 1

All telephone marketing contacts should promptly disclose the name of the sponsor and the primary purpose(s) of the contact. No one should make offers or solicitations in the guise of research or a survey when the real intent is to sell products or services or to raise funds.

Honesty
Article 2

All offers should be clear, honest and complete so that the recipient of the call will know the exact nature of what is being offered and the commitment involved in the placing of an order. Before making an offer, direct marketers should be prepared to substantiate any claims or offers made. Advertisements or specific claims which are untrue, misleading, deceptive, fraudulent, or unjustly disparaging of competitors should not be used. All documents confirming the transactions should contain the means for the consumer to contact the telephone marketer.

Terms
Article 3

Prior to commitments by customers, all telephone marketers should disclose the cost of the merchandise or service, all terms, conditions, payment plans and the amount or existence of any extra charges such as shipping and handling.

Reasonable Hours
Article 4

Telephone marketers should avoid making contacts during hours which are unreasonable to the recipients of the calls.

Use Of Automatic Equipment
Article 5

No telephone marketer should solicit sales using automatic dialing equipment unless the telephone immediately releases the line when the called party disconnects.

Telephone marketers should not use such devices as automatic dialers and pre-recorded messages when in violation of tariffs, state or local laws, or these Guidelines.

When a marketer places a call to an individual as part of a solicitation process, and desires to deliver a recorded message to that individual, permission should be obtained from the individual by a live "operator" before the recorded message is delivered.

Taping Of Conversations
Article 6

Taping of telephone conversations should be conducted only with all-party consent or the use of a beeping device.

Name Removal
Article 7

Telephone marketers should remove the name of any contact from their telephone lists when requested to do so.

When possible, telephone marketers should offer to remove consumers' names from lists that are offered to other telephone marketers.

Minors
Article 8

Because minors are generally less experienced in their rights as consumers, telephone marketers should be especially sensitive to the obligations and responsibilities involved when dealing with them.

Prompt Delivery
Article 9

Telephone marketers should abide by the FTC's Mail Order Merchandise (30 Day) Rule when shipping prepaid merchandise.

As a normal business procedure, telephone marketers are urged to ship all orders as soon as practical.

Cooling-Off Period
Article 10

Telephone marketers should honor cancellation requests which originate within three days of sales agreements.

Restricted Contacts
Article 11

Telephone marketers should avoid calling telephone subscribers who have unlisted or unpublished telephone numbers unless a prior relationship exists.

Random dialing techniques, where indentification of those parties to be called is left to chance, should not be used in sales and marketing situations, whether a manual or automated process.

Sequential dialing techniques, where selection of those parties to be called is based on the location of their telephone number in a sequence of telephone numbers, should not be used, whether a manual or automated process.

Laws Codes And Regulations
Article 12

Telephone marketers should operate in accordance with the laws and regulations of the United States Postal Service, the

Federal Communications Commission, the Federal Trade Commission, the Federal Reserve Board and other applicable Federal, state and local laws governing advertising, marketing practices and the transaction of business by mail, telephone, and the print and broadcast media.

For additional information contact:
Ethics Department
Direct Marketing Association, Inc.
6 East 43rd Street, New York, NY 10017
(212) 689-4977
•
1101 17th Street, N.W., Suite 900
Washington, DC 20036
(202) 347-1222

Index

Selected Listing of Suppliers
to the
Telemarketing Industry

ACDs

Rockwell International
Switching Systems Division
1431 Opus Place
Downers Grove, IL 60515
312/960-8400

Teknekron Infoswitch
P.O. Box 61247
D/FW Airport, TX 75261
817/354-0661

Telcom Technologies
3072 East G. Street
Ontario, CA 91764
714/980-5000

Automated Telemarketing — Hardware

Commercial Data Systems Corporation
2812 New Spring Road
Suite 100
Atlanta, GA 30339
404/436-6565

Rockwell International
Switching Systems Division
1431 Opus Place
Downers Grove, IL 60515
312/960-8400

Automated Telemarketing — Software

Arlington Software & Systems Corp.
Telemarketing Division
400 Massachusetts Avenue
Arlington, MA 02174
617/641-0290

Commercial Data Systems Corporation
2812 New Spring Road
Suite 100
Atlanta, GA 30339
404/436-6565

Rockwell International
Switching Systems Division
1431 Opus Place
Downers Grove, IL 60515
312/960-8400

Automated Telemarketing — Turnkey

Commercial Data Systems Corporation
2812 New Spring Road
Suite 100
Atlanta, GA 30339
404/436-6565

Dialogic Communications Corporation
P.O. Box 8
1106 Harpeth Industrial Court
Franklin, TN 37064
800/553-8505

Rockwell International
Switching Systems Division
1431 Opus Place
Downers Grove, IL 60515
312/960-8400

Teknekron Infoswitch
P.O. Box 61247
D/FW Airport, TX 75261
817/354-0661

Call Accounting Equipment

Newcastle Communications
270 Lafayette Street
Suite 904
New York, NY 10012
212/431-7220

Call Accounting Services

Newcastle Communications
270 Lafayette Street
Suite 904
New York, NY 10012
212/431-7220

Custom Calling Services

**Bell of Pennsylvania/
Diamond State Telephone**
One Presidential Boulevard
Second Floor
Bala Cynwyd, PA 19004
800/843-2255

C&P Telephone
Business Communications
Center
11710 Beltsville Drive
Second Floor
Beltsville, MD 20705
800/843-2255

New Jersey Bell
114 Midland Avenue
Kearny, NJ 07032
800/843-2255

Direct Marketing Services

**Sell Smart Telemarketing
and Customer Relations
Workshops**
C&P Telephone
11710 Beltsville Drive
Second Floor
Beltsville, MD 20705
800/843-2255

**Sell Smart Telemarketing
and Customer Relations
Workshops**
Bell of Pennsylvania/
Diamond State Telephone
One Presidential Blvd.
Second Floor
Bala Cynwyd, PA 19004
800/843-2255

**Sell Smart Telemarketing
and Customer Relations
Workshops**
New Jersey Bell
Gateway Two
Arcade Level
Newark, NJ 07102
800/843-2255

Headsets

ACS Communications, Inc.
250 Technology Circle
Scotts Valley, CA 95066
800/538-0742 or
408/438-3883 Inside CA

Danavox, Inc.
Telecommunications Division
6400 Flying Cloud Drive
Minneapolis, MN 55344
800/328-6297 or
612/941-0690

Plantronics/Santa Cruz
345 Encinal Street
Santa Cruz, CA 95060
800/662-3902 Inside CA
800/538-0748 Outside CA

Long-Distance Services

Jersey-Link
Bell of Pennsylvania
841 Chestnut Street
10th Floor
Philadelphia, PA 19107
800/742-5272

VIP
Bell of Pennsylvania
One Presidential Blvd.
Second Floor
Bala Cynwyd, PA 19004
800/843-2255

WATS
Bell of Pennsylvania
One Presidential Blvd.
Second Floor
Bala Cynwyd, PA 19004
800/843-2255

WATS
New Jersey Bell
Gateway Two
Arcade Level
Newark, NJ 07102
800/843-2255

Sales Training Programs

CCI Telemarketing Corporation
555 West 57th Street
New York, NY 10019
800/528-7785

Learning International
Formerly Xerox
Learning Systems
P.O. Box 10211
Stamford, CT 06904
203/965-8444

Sell Smart Telemarketing and Customer Relations Workshops
C&P Telephone
11710 Beltsville Drive
Second Floor
Beltsville, MD 20705
800/843-2255

Sell Smart Telemarketing and Customer Relations Workshops
Bell of Pennsylvania/
Diamond State Telephone
One Presidential Blvd.
Second Floor
Bala Cynwyd, PA 19004
800/843-2255

Sell Smart Telemarketing and Customer Relations Workshops
New Jersey Bell
Gateway Two
Arcade Level
Newark, NJ 07102
800/843-2255

Telespectrum, Inc.
406 Headquarters Drive
Millersville, MD 21108
800/824-1774 or
301/987-7300

SMDR

Newcastle Communications
270 Lafayette Street
Suite 904
New York, NY 10012
212/431-7220

Switching Systems

Rockwell International
Switching Systems Division
1431 Opus Place
Downers Grove, IL 60515
312/960-8400

Telemarketing Consulting Services

CCI Telemarketing Corporation
555 West 57th Street
New York, NY 10019
800/528-7785

Edward Blank Associates, Inc.
71 West 23rd Street
New York, NY 10010
212/741-8133 or
800/ED-BLANK

Institute for Marketing Specialists
P.O. Box 963
Burlington, MA 01803
617/272-1438

Sell Smart Telemarketing And Customer Relations Workshops
C&P Telephone
11710 Beltsville Drive
Second Floor
Beltsville, MD 20705
800/843-2255

Sell Smart Telemarketing
And Customer Relations
Workshops
Bell of Pennsylvania/
Diamond State Telephone
One Presidential Blvd.
Second Floor
Bala Cynwyd, PA 19004
800/843-2255

Sell Smart Telemarketing
And Customer Relations
Workshops
New Jersey Bell
Gateway Two
Arcade Level
Newark, NJ 07102
800/843-2255

Telespectrum, Inc.
406 Headquarters Drive
Millersville, MD 21108
800/824-1774 or
301/987-7300

Telemarketing Services

CCI Telemarketing
Corporation
555 West 57th Street
New York, NY 10019
800/528-7785

Edward Blank
Associates, Inc.
71 West 23rd Street
New York, NY 10010
212/741-8133 or
800/ED-BLANK

Institute for Marketing
Specialists
P.O. Box 963
Burlington, MA 01803
617/272-1438

Call Center Services
302 Knickerbocker Road
Cresskill, NJ 07626
800/238-CALL or
800/238-2254 in NJ

National Systems
Corporation
65 Jackson Drive
Suite 2000
Cranford, NJ 07016
201/272-0428

Sell Smart Telemarketing
And Customer Relations
Workshops
C&P Telephone
11710 Beltsville Drive
Second Floor
Beltsville, MD 20705
800/843-2255

Sell Smart Telemarketing
And Customer Relations
Workshops
Bell of Pennsylvania/
Diamond State Telephone
One Presidential Blvd.
Second Floor
Bala Cynwyd, PA 19004
800/843-2255

Sell Smart Telemarketing
And Customer Relations
Workshops
New Jersey Bell
Gateway Two
Arcade Level
Newark, NJ 07102
800/843-2255

Tele America Inc.
1955 Raymond Drive
Suite 112
Northbrook, IL 60062
312/480-1560

Trans World Telesystems, Inc.
65 Jackson Drive
Suite 2000
Cranford, NJ 07016
201/272-1062

Video Training Programs

Coronet/MTI Film & Video
Div. of Simon & Schuster
108 Wilmot Road
Deerfield, IL 60015
312/940-1260

Telemarketing Isn't Like 'Dialing For Dollars'

At times your phone room can seem like a Dialing for Dollars Show, instead of the serious business you want it to be... Salespeople dialing slowly (or not at all), unpredictable contact rates, high turnover, unmanageable call programs and worse.

The result is a low completed call rate and lost sales.

A Call Management System from Trans World Telesystems will help you recover this lost productivity. In fact, our systems can boost completed call rates by as much as 300 percent by keeping your operators on the line all the time.

A TWT System automatically surveys your prospect data base and dials out on up to 12 lines simultaneously. When a voice response is detected, the live call is forwarded to an operator, eliminating wasted time.

At the same time, the prospect's record is displayed for the operator, allowing immediate order entry and record updating. When the call is completed, the new record is returned to the data base. "No answer" and "busy" calls are recycled for later attempts.

At the end of a shift, the system can automatically generate a call report and order files on virtually any media, including printouts, mag-tape and/or direct mainframe update. This eliminates the need for manually written call reports and sales orders.

TWT's Call Management Systems can increase your profit margins through increased calling rates, lower overhead and increased sales. They can be integrated with your present mainframe or operate independently. "User-friendly" software keeps training to a minimum. And we offer an exceptional program of technical and software support.

Our systems design staff is available for a no-obligation analysis of your current call program. Contact our sales office for details.

Because your phone room is no place to play Dialing-for-Dollars.

Trans World Telesystems, Inc.
Trans World Telephone, Inc.
National Systems Corporation

65 Jackson Drive, Suite 2000, Cranford, NJ 07016
Telex: 5101010207   1-(201)-272-1062

YOUR PLACE OR OURS?

OUR PLACE. Regardless of which decision maker you need to reach, we can develop your strategies, create your scripts, generate qualified leads, and close the sales. Just ask **IBM, Polaroid Corporation**, and **Citibank**. When they needed a top telemarketer, they came to CCI. After all, we defined the industry over 20 years ago.

YOUR PLACE. If you're just starting up your own in-house facility, our **Needs Analysis** will save you from some of the pitfalls. Or, if you have your operation in place already, our one-day **Telemarketing Tune-Up** will help you protect your investment. Our Consultants can measure your performance levels and know how to diagnose a problem. We'll prescribe the most effective remedy to keep you running at peak efficiency.

Either way, call us.

212-957-8520
800-528-7785

Telemarketing
555 W. 57th St.
NY, NY 10019

YOUR BEST SALES PRO

It's been in your business since day one. And you pay for it every month, but it probably spends the workday just hanging around, waiting for someone to call. That's a shame. Because if your salespeople put it to work, it can deliver more business in one day than you might generate in a week. Get it moving and it will give you statewide sales in the time you spend on a single deal. A list of leads today, turns into a column of profits tomorrow. Trouble is, it's no good at all unless you put it in the right hands, and aim it in the right direction.

Your Telemarketing Source For Over 35 Years. Convenience and experience...when and where you need it.

Now Bell Atlantic has put all of its tested, on-target research, solid experience and expertise into four competitively priced Telemarketing and Customer Relations Workshops. Workshops especially designed to show you how to make your telephone the most productive part of your business.

Four dynamic, interactive workshops, located in your area, and conveniently arranged to suit your schedule and business needs. Each one is geared to show you and your staff how your phone can become the best salesperson, collector, and customer liaison you've ever seen.

The convenient way to telemarketing expertise. At enrollment fees you and your company can live with. Our ongoing regional schedules include:

- Telemarketing Manager's Workshop—to get your Center started.
- Telemarketing Sales Representative Training—for increased profits through the use of proven sales skills.
- Telecollections—turn accounts receivable into positive cash flow.
- Teleprofessionalism—company reputation, the telephone, and the bottom line.

Sell Smart℠ Workshops are accredited for Continuing Education Units.

Call us today or write to Bell Atlantic, Telemarketing Division, 8th Floor, Attn: K. Koontz, 1310 North Court House Road, Arlington, VA 22201 for more information on enrollment fees and workshop registration. Put your best sales pro to work, by getting your phone off the hook.

1 800 843-2255, ext. 607

(Within the Bell Atlantic territory)
(9 a.m. to 5 p.m. Monday-Friday)

SELL SMART
Telemarketing and Customer Relations Workshops

**Bell of Pennsylvania
C&P Telephone
Diamond State Telephone
New Jersey Bell**
Bell Atlantic™ Companies

To Order Back Issues . . .
Or To Subscribe,
Call TOLL-FREE

800-243-6002